LIBROS

W9-AQH-012

LA CUCARACHA: THE FIRST COLLECTION FROM THE DAILY COMIC STRIP BY LALO ALCARAZ

BARRIO BUGLE

PHILLIES

CHUY'S

CHECK CASHING AND PLASTIC SURGERY

POCHO

To Gus Arriola, Sergio Aragones, Ruis, Los Hernandez Bros, Quino, and all the unsung cartoonistas in Latin America

LA CUCARACHA

LALO ALCARAZ

Andrews McMeel
Publishing

Kansas City

———— **ATTENTION: SCHOOLS AND BUSINESSES** ————

Andrews McMeel books are available at quantity discounts with bulk purchase for educational, business, or sales promotional use. For information, please write to: Special Sales Department, Andrews McMeel Publishing, 4520 Main Street, Kansas City, Missouri 64111.

Introducing *La Cucaracha*

(This review by comics scholar R. C. Harvey first appeared in the *Comics Journal* 2002 Review of the Year.)

The latest entry into the lists of deliberately antagonistic comic strips is *La Cucaracha*, a Latino land mine planted in the Hispanic boondocks, by Lalo Alcaraz, a 38-year-old comedian, writer, illustrator, political agitator, public speaker, and cartoonist. It is no coincidence that Alcaraz's strip is syndicated by Universal Press, which also distributes *The Boondocks* and *Doonesbury*, as well as *Baldo*, a strip launched in 2000 about an agreeable Latino teenager and his family by Hector Cantú and artist Carlos Castellanos. Looking at this lineup, you'd think Universal has a corner on the controversy market. It also distributes Pat Oliphant's ferocious editorial cartoon as well as Ted Rall's endeavors.

The comics pages need sharp-edged, culturally critical voices, says Greg Melvin, who is Aaron McGruder's and Alcaraz's editor at Universal. "The comics have to reflect the world is changing."

Alcaraz's parents were Mexican natives but he was born and educated in the U.S., spending summers in Mexico, where he was exposed to that country's prolific cartoon industry, which produces comic book print runs in the millions. At San Diego State University, Alcaraz drew editorial cartoons for the campus paper, graduating in 1987 and going to UC Berkeley to pursue a master's degree in architecture. There, he cofounded a comedy sketch troupe, the Chicano Secret Service, that toured the West Coast 1988–1996, and a satirical 'zine, *Pocho*. Since 1992, he has produced editorial cartoons for the *L.A. Weekly*, and that's where his cockroach debuted as "L.A. Cucaracha."

The unruly insect was featured in the early strips but faded into the background somewhat as the strip slowly transformed itself into a single-panel editorial cartoon. Alcaraz, meanwhile, approached several syndicates with a proposal to do a comic strip based upon the character. In 1998, Universal signed him to a development contract that gave him time and editorial guidance in refining his concept. That *The Boondocks* was launched at right about that time is probably not coincidental: McGruder's strip enjoyed the most successful launch in recent history, strenuously suggesting, I surmise, that something appealing to the growing Latino population in the U.S. might also do well.

Although well-received in various markets, *Baldo*, Universal's first foray in this direction, is too good-natured to swagger up to Hispanic readership the way *The Boondocks* did to African-American readership everywhere it appeared. *La Cucaracha*, however, is right on target. (Alcaraz jokingly calls it "Doonesbarrio.")

The chief actors in the strip's inaugural weeks are Eddie, an easy-going Mexican American (who might be Alcaraz's milder alter ego) with whom the title character (aka Cuco Rocha, an anthropomorphic hipster of the Blattidae persuasion, the cartoonist's politically radical side) bickers about the state of Latino America; Neto, Eddie's tech-savvy bicultural little brother; and Vero (for Veronica), a Latina with her head on straight who might be the only sensible one of the bunch.

Alcaraz's drawing style, simple and somewhat angular with an unvarying line, is entirely competent, betraying actual artistic skill (unusual among so many contemporary newspaper strips). He spots blacks nicely, and the strip has a crisp attractive clarity. His images, particularly Vero's, sometimes, perhaps unintentionally, evoke Mexican codex. Often (but not always) he devotes most of every panel to the utterances of his characters with the result that much of the humor is verbal, the pictures serving merely to identify the speakers and time comedic revelations.

Alcaraz chose a cockroach as his title character because, he told me, he "didn't want to toss away a character that my audience was familiar with."

By using *la cucaracha*, a traditional literary figure in Mexican pop culture, Alcaraz also strikes a blow for Latino status by turning a negative into a positive.

Said Alcaraz: "In the U.S., the cockroach was turned into a racial epithet by Americans (who will swear up and down that there is no racism in this country) against Mexicans, Chicanos, and Latinos alike. I reclaim the cucaracha," he continued [I can almost see him mounting the barricade, waving a banner], "which has come to represent the people, the masses, the lumpen, the underdog, and have put him on top. He is defiant and makes the statement—Yeah, I'm a cucaracha! What are you gonna do about it?"

Said Alcaraz: "Latinos don't ingest enough irony."

He acknowledges "a lot of people get on me for criticizing Latinos, but I always say I do it because I care."

But "someone had to make a big splash and create a strip that makes a statement, that takes a stand, and has the nerve to disagree with the mainstream. I'm here to make an impact."

At the same time, he aims to "create images and portrayals of Latinos and other people of color in the media that don't come off as stereotypes, or sunny, Pollyanna-ish idealized caricatures of real people. Latinos are normal people. We are so mainstream it's ridiculous. I want to show how we speak Spanglish, how we relate to stuff on TV, how we feel alienated, and how we like watching *Friends*."

In short, Alcaraz will be lobbing satiric grenades over the fence in both directions—at the American and Latino mainstreams.

Panel 1: LATE ONE NIGHT, YET ANOTHER COMIC STRIP IS BORN.

Panel 2: EDDIE! NO COFFEE, NO CARTOON!

Panel 3: WAIT A SEC-YOU'RE NOT REAL! YOU'RE JUST A CARTOON COCKROACH-THIS IS NO PLACE FOR YOU!

Panel 4: TELL ME ABOUT IT. WHAT A DUMP.

11/25

©2002 LALO ALCARAZ /Dist. by Universal Press Syndicate

Panel 5: SO WHAT'S OUR STORY? HOW CAN I EXPLAIN YOU ARE A HUMAN-SIZED ANTHROPOMORPHIC CUCARACHA?

Panel 6: WERE YOU CREATED BY A MAD SCIENTIST? NO, WAIT! YOU WERE BITTEN BY A RADIO-ACTIVE ROACH?!

Panel 7: JUST TELL 'EM THE TRUTH— I'M YOUR RADICALLY POLITICAL ALTER EGO—A COCKROACH—A TRADITIONAL LITERARY FIGURE IN MEXICAN POP CULTURE MEANT TO EVOKE THE MASSES, THE PEOPLE, **LA RAZA!** A CREATURE CONSTANTLY CRUSHED-IN FUTILITY-BY **THE MAN!!**

Panel 8: HOW ABOUT, "HE ATE A TACO SOAKED IN **RAID** $_{TM}$?"

11/26

©2002 LALO ALCARAZ /Dist. by Universal Press Syndicate

Panel 9: AS YOUR ALTER EGO, IT'S MY DUTY TO EXPLAIN THAT I'VE LEAPT OFF THE PAGE AND RIGHT INTO YOUR BORING LIFE.

WHAT A CHEAP STORY DEVICE!

Panel 10: EDDIE, YOU'RE LATINO, RIGHT? JUST SAY IT'S "**MAGICAL REALISM**," THE USE OF FANTASTICAL, DREAMLIKE IMAGERY FOUND IN SOME LATIN AMERICAN LITERATURE.

Panel 11: ¡PÚF!

Panel 12: "MAGICAL REALISM" IS ALSO A CHEAP STORY DEVICE.

SHUT UP AND START FLAPPING.

11/27

©2002 LALO ALCARAZ /Dist. by Universal Press Syndicate

7

Panel 1: BUT CUCO, YOU'RE A COCKROACH! / YEAH, I GOT THE MEMO.

Panel 2: DON'T YOU THINK THAT'S GOING TO BE DIFFICULT FOR SOME PEOPLE TO ACCEPT? / BELIEVE ME, NO ONE WILL NOTICE!

Panel 3: SOMEWHERE IN AMERICA... / LOOK DEAR, A BUG-EYED LATINO HAS JUST GOTTEN HIS OWN COMIC STRIP. / I'LL WRITE THE COMPLAINT LETTER! / 11/28

Panel 4: YOU GUYS ARE ALWAYS JUST SITTING HERE! DO YOU WANT PEOPLE TO THINK YOU'RE LAZY? / 11/29

Panel 5: VERO, IF WE WERE WHITE, WE WOULDN'T BE "LAZY"...

Panel 6: WE'D BE "SLACKERS."

Panel 7: TV IS ROTTING YOUR MINDS. WHY DON'T YOU GUYS GET UP AND DO SOMETHING OUTSIDE!? / 11/30

Panel 8: YOU'RE RIGHT, VERO. BESIDES, THERE'S NOTHING ON EXCEPT SOME DUMB INTERVIEW WITH OSCAR DE LA HOYA AND BENJAMIN BRATT FROLICKING ON THE BEACH...

©2002 LALO ALCARAZ /Dist. by Universal Press Syndicate

8

YO QUIERO ENGLISH ONLY.

TACOS

ENGLISH ONLY FOUNDATION

PLEASE SIGN MY PETITION TO MAKE ENGLISH THE OFFICIAL LANGUAGE.

NO WAY, JOSÉ! WHY SHOULD I SIGN THAT?!

MY GROUP FEELS ENGLISH IS THE ONLY WAY ALL AMERICANS CAN COMMUNICATE WITH EACH OTHER.

ADIOS!

WAIT AMIGOS!

WE MUST PRESERVE THE PURITY OF THE ENGLISH LANGUAGE.

WHOA, DEJA VU!

TOO MUCH DIVERSITY LEADS TO CONFLICT.

WHAT TYPE OF CONFLICT?

MANO A MANO TYPE CONFLICT.

GET A GRIP! THIS COUNTRY IS STRONGER BECAUSE OF THE CONTRIBUTIONS OF DIFFERENT CULTURES—AND GUESS WHAT? SPANGLISH IS ALREADY AMERICA'S UNOFFICIAL, OFFICIAL LANGUAGE!

NO MAS! NO MAS!

SO IF YOU CAN'T SEE THAT, THEN HASTA LA VISTA, BABY!

LALO ALCARAZ

12/1

THAT GUY IS LOCO EN LA CABEZA!

FOUNDATION

©2002 LALO ALCARAZ /Dist. by Universal Press Syndicate

9

Strip 1 (12/2): TITANS

"BY THE YEAR 2050, LATINOS WILL OUTNUMBER EVERYONE ELSE." / "SO?" / CENSUS

"SO?! IT MEANS LATINOS WILL BE IN CHARGE AND WE'LL RUN THINGS OUR WAY!"

2050 →

"CUCO, REMEMBER HOW IT WAS BEFORE THEY SHIPPED ALL THE LATINOS TO THE MOON?"

Strip 2 (12/3):

"'THE CENSUS RESULTS INDICATE THE LATINO POPULATION WILL BE RECEIVING A LOT MORE ATTENTION.'" / LAS NEWS

"WOW! IT'S LIKE WE'RE FINALLY BEING DISCOVERED!"

"YEAH, EDDIE, 'BEING DISCOVERED' REALLY WORKED OUT WELL FOR THE INDIANS."

Strip 3 (12/4):

"ANOTHER DOWNSIDE TO LATINOS BECOMING THE BIGGEST MINORITY IS THE ENDLESS CHEESY MARKETING." / "I HATE THAT!" / LAS NEWS!

"HOW ARE YOU GUYS GONNA PAY TONIGHT?" / CUENTA

"COOL, I'LL USE MY NEW RICKY MARTIN VISA CARD!"

©2002 LALO ALCARAZ / Dist. by Universal Press Syndicate

LALO ALCARAZ

10

TITANS
©2002 LALO ALCARAZ /Dist. by Universal Press Syndicate
CHECK THIS OUT. THE CENSUS SHOWS THAT LATINOS ARE NOW THE NATION'S LARGEST MINORITY...
LAS NEWS
12/5
WHO WAS THE LARGEST MINORITY BEFORE?
SHAQUILLE O'NEAL!
LALO ALCARAZ

DON'T BE SO CYNICAL, CUCO. AMERICA JUST **LOVES** LATINOS NOW!
©2002 LALO ALCARAZ /Dist. by Universal Press Syndicate
DIDN'T YOU KNOW? **SALSA** OUTSELLS KETCHUP IN THE USA!
12/6
YEAH, EDDIE, AND RAP OUTSELLS ROCK. BUT YOU DON'T SEE GWYNETH PALTROW DATING SNOOP DOGG...
LALO ALCARAZ

MR. CARTOONIST,
I AM WRITING TO COMPLAIN ABOUT THE NAME OF YOUR COMIC STRIP "**LA CUCARACHA.**"
LALO ALCARAZ
BY USING A FILTHY ANIMAL SUCH AS A COCKROACH, YOU ARE IMPLYING THAT LATINOS ARE INSECTS. THIS PERPETUATES NEGATIVE STEREOTYPES OF LATINOS.
©2002 LALO ALCARAZ /Dist. by Universal Press Syndicate
SINCERELY, A CONCERNED BUSINESS OWNER,
NORA SANCHEZ
PROPRIETOR,
EL GORDO BANDIDO
RESTAURANT
12/7

Panel 1: "FRIENDS" IS ON. — I HEARD "FRIENDS" IS FEATURING A REVAMPED URBAN SETTING WITH ACTUAL MINORITIES. — STAY TUNED FOR THE REVAMPED "FRIENDS," NOW RENAMED "WHITE FLIGHT."

Panel 2: BARRIO BUCKS CAFE — EDDIE! HOW CAN YOU WATCH "FRIENDS"? THEY LIVE IN NEW YORK BUT IT LOOKS MORE LIKE STOCKHOLM!

Panel 3: I GUESS SO. THERE COULD BE MORE PEOPLE OF COLOR ON ALL TV SHOWS... — YEAH... THERE'S NO "AMIGOS" ON "FRIENDS."

Panel 4: HEY! YOU'RE A REVERSE RACIST! YOU WANT MORE MINORITIES ON TV, BUT THERE'S ALREADY **TELEMUNDO** AND **UNIVISION** FOR HISPANICS—AND WHAT ABOUT **B.E.T.** FOR BLACKS?!

Panel 5: SHOULDN'T THERE BE A "WHITE ENTERTAINMENT INDUSTRY"?! — 12/8

Panel 6: THERE IS...

Panel 7: IT'S CALLED "HOLLYWOOD." — LALO ALCARAZ

©2002 LALO ALCARAZ /Dist by Universal Press Syndicate

12

Row 1:

Panel 1: LA CUCARACHA'S **BEHIND THE ANIMAL**™ PRESENTS: **THE TACO BOWL CHIHUAHUA** TONIGHT "THE FAST AND THE FURRIEST"

Panel 2: HE WAS ONCE THE MOST RECOGNIZED LATINO IN AMERICA.

Panel 3: HIS HEAVILY ACCENTED SPEECH AND UBIQUITOUS CATCHPHRASE HELPED SELL A BILLION BLAND "BEEF-A-RITOS!" — "YO QUIERO TACO BOWL"

Panel 4: BUT IT ALL FELL APART FASTER THAN A PIÑATA AT A BARRIO BIRTHDAY PARTY... WHO LET ME OUT? WOOF WOOF WOOF WOOF WHO LET 12/9

Row 2:

Panel 1: LA CUCARACHA'S **BEHIND THE ANIMAL**™ PRESENTS: **THE TACO BOWL CHIHUAHUA** TONIGHT "CATACLYSM"

Panel 2: I BLEW MY MONEY ON GOLD-PLATED FIRE HYDRANTS... I EVEN HAD A HOUSE ON THE EAST AND WEST SIDE OF THE YARD. 12/10

Panel 3: I RAN AROUND WITH A DIFFERENT POODLE EVERY NIGHT...

Panel 4: I EVEN DABBLED WITH... CATS!

Row 3:

Panel 1: LA CUCARACHA'S **BEHIND THE ANIMAL**™ PRESENTS: **THE TACO BOWL CHIHUAHUA** TONIGHT "IT'S LIKE MEXICAN FOOD"

Panel 2: I HAD SUNK SO LOW THAT THEY STOPPED PAYING ME IN CASH...

Panel 3: SOON THEY WERE PAYING ME IN... TACO BOWL FAST FOOD!

Panel 4: IT TASTES JUST LIKE DOG FOOD! 12/11

©2002 LALO ALCARAZ /Dist. by Universal Press Syndicate

LALO ALCARAZ

13

LA CUCARACHA'S **BEHIND THE ANIMAL** ™ PRESENTS: **THE TACO BOWL CHIHUAHUA** TONIGHT "GOOD BOY"

THE FAST LIFE FINALLY CAUGHT THE TACO BOWL CHIHUAHUA BY THE TAIL...

SNARED IN AN INSIDER TRADING SCANDAL, HE WAS SENTENCED TO SERVE 18 MONTHS IN A COUNTY ANIMAL DETENTION CENTER. 24782321 12/12

BUT FORTUNATELY, HE WAS AWARDED AN EARLY RELEASE FOR GOOD BEHAVIOR. SIT! FETCH! ROLL OVER!

YO QUIERO TACO BOWL.

YO QUIERO TACO BOWL. 12/13

YO QUIERO TACO BOWL!

¡CHIHUAHUA! DOESN'T ANYONE SPEAK ENGLISH AROUND HERE?

WILL ENDORSE YOUR PRODUCT FOR FOOD 12/14

EDDIE, LOOK, IT'S THE TACO BOWL CHIHUAHUA... HOW THE MIGHTY HAVE FALLEN!

YO QUIERO SPARE CHANGE!

©2002 LALO ALCARAZ /Dist. by Universal Press Syndicate

14

©2002 LALO ALCARAZ /Dist. by Universal Press Syndicate

EL MIGRA

LALO ALCARAZ

LAZY IMMIGRANT!

12/15

15

Panel 1 (12/16): WHERE ARE ALL THE MINORITIES ON THE NEW PRIME-TIME TV SEASON? ALSO IN HONOR OF HISPANIC HERITAGE MONTH...

Panel 2: THE FIRST LATINO POLICE DRAMA ON PRIME-TIME TV— HOLD IT, BRO, THIS SOUNDS GOOD...

Panel 3: PUERTO RICO PD STARRING THE OLSEN TWINS

Panel 4 (12/17): TONIGHT! ON "BLONDE AND SINGLE IN MANHATTAN"! HAVE YOU NOTICED HOW THERE ARE SO FEW MINORITIES ON TV?

Panel 5: THERE ARE PLENTY OF MINORITIES ON TV. YOU'RE JUST NOT WATCHING THE RIGHT CHANNELS. OH YEAH? SHOW ME...

Panel 6: TONIGHT! ON THE "70s CHANNEL — CHICO AND THE MAN"! WOW! THIS IS GREAT! CHECK OUT MY NEW GOAT, CHICO! LOOOOOK-EEEENG GOOOOD!

Panel 7 (12/18): CUCO, WE JUST WASTED A WHOLE NIGHT COMPLAINING ABOUT THE LACK OF LATINOS AND MINORITIES ON PRIME-TIME TV! HARLEM HIGH STARRING BRITNEY SPEARS!

Panel 8: FORGET THE TUBE, WE SHOULD DO SOME READING INSTEAD... KLIK

Panel 9: WHATTYA GOT? A WHOLE MONTH OF TV GUIDE!

©2002 LALO ALCARAZ /Dist. by Universal Press Syndicate

16

Strip 1 (12/19):

CUCO and EDDIE PROTEST THE LACK OF MINORITIES ON TV BY DOING A LITTLE READING...

MY TV GUIDE™ SAYS NETWORKS ARE ADDING NEW ETHNIC CHARACTERS TO EXISTING TV SHOWS.

LET'S WATCH **THOSE** SHOWS!

HERE'S ONE: "A POPULAR SITCOM ADDS A YOUNG LATINO TO ITS ALL-WHITE CAST."

KUK

TV GUIDE — NEW FALL SEASON

TONIGHT ON "JUST SHOOT HIM"...

©2002 LALO ALCARAZ /Dist. by Universal Press Syndicate

Strip 2 (12/20):

TONIGHT ON "**JUST SHOOT HIM**"—THE CAST WELCOMES THE NEW TOKEN LATINO!

LET ME FIND ANOTHER SHOW WITH A NEW LATINO CAST MEMBER.

CLEEK

"A MEXICAN IMMIGRANT JOINS THE CAST OF THIS HIGHLY RATED FAMILY SITCOM."

LALO ALCARAZ

STAY TUNED FOR "EVERYBODY HATES RAMON."

©2002 LALO ALCARAZ /Dist. by Universal Press Syndicate

Strip 3 (12/21):

POST OFFICE

JOVEN, ¿ME PUEDE DECIR QUE DICE ESTA CARTA?

NETO, SHE NEEDS A TRANSLATION OF THIS LETTER...

LET ME TRY.

LALO ALCARAZ

ESTA-LETTER -IS-UN-UH -BILL-O-DE -GASS-O...

DUDE, I CAN'T EVEN SPEAK "**SPANGLISH.**" IT'S MORE LIKE "**MANGLE-ISH!**"

©2002 LALO ALCARAZ /Dist. by Universal Press Syndicate

17

I'M DREAMING OF A WHIIIIITE CHRISTMAS...

HOLD ON! THAT'S BEEN DECLARED ILLEGAL BY THE SUPREME COURT!

DO YOU THINK THAT'LL STAND WITH THE REPUBLICAN-CONTROLLED CONGRESS??

IS IT WRONG TO DREAM OF A BROWN CHRISTMAS?

CAN WE HAVE A NORMAL HOLIDAY JUST ONCE?!

©2002 LALO ALCARAZ /Dist. by Universal Press Syndicate

18

Strip 1 (12/23):

Panel 1: LET'S GO TO TITAN'S CANTINA FOR A COLDIE! YEAH!

Panel 2: TITAN'S LIKE A TOTAL IMMIGRANT SUCCESS STORY! TOO BAD HE HAD TO LEAVE HIS WRESTLING CAREER IN MEXICO.

Panel 3: EXCUSE, ME BOYS. I NEED TO ESCORT THIS FELLOW OUT OF THE RING.

©2002 LALO ALCARAZ /Dist. by Universal Press Syndicate

LALO ALCARAZ

Strip 2 (12/24):

Panel 1: WHEN DID YOU IMMIGRATE, TITAN? UUF. WHEN I WAS A YOUNG LUCHADOR. I WAS GOING TO MAKE IT BIG IN AMERICAN WRESTLING... CHELAS

Panel 2: THEN I WAS GOING TO CASH IN AND TRIUMPHANTLY RETURN TO MEXICO... WHAT HAPPENED?

Panel 3: MEXICO CAME TO ME. Pisto

©2002 LALO ALCARAZ /Dist. by Universal Press Syndicate

LALO ALCARAZ

Strip 3 (12/25):

Panel 1: LOOK, YOU HAVE TO AGREE THAT IMMIGRANTS ARE TAKING JOBS FROM AMERICANS!

Panel 2: WHEN'S THE LAST TIME YOU WORKED PICKING LETTUCE IN THE FIELDS? WELL, NEVER.

Panel 3: WE HAVE IMMIGRANTS TO DO **THAT** KIND OF WORK! CERVEZA

©2002 LALO ALCARAZ /Dist. by Universal Press Syndicate

LALO ALCARAZ

19

Panel 1: I'M TELLING YA, THERE'S TOO MANY IMMIGRANTS POURING INTO THIS COUNTRY! THAT'S WHY THINGS ARE SO BAD IN AMERICA!
FRIA

Panel 2: BARTENDER, ANOTHER DRINK! — HEY, BUDDY, I'M AN IMMIGRANT, AND GUESS WHAT?
12/26

Panel 3: WHAT? — I'M NOT POURING.
LALO ALCARAZ

©2002 LALO ALCARAZ /Dist. by Universal Press Syndicate

Panel 4: HEY, VERO, WHAT ARE YOU GUYS WATCHING? — SOME REALITY SHOW.

Panel 5: WHY DO THEY CALL THEM "REALITY SHOWS"? THEY NEVER HAVE LATINOS ON THEM! THEY SHOULD BE CALLED "UNREALITY SHOWS." — SHHHH!
12/27

Panel 6: IF I RAN TELEVISION, I'D MAKE SOME RADICAL CHANGES IN THE SYSTEM! — IF YOU RAN TELEVISION, I'D RUN FOR THE BOOKSTORE.
LALO ALCARAZ

©2002 LALO ALCARAZ /Dist. by Universal Press Syndicate

CUCO IMAGINES WHAT HE'D DO IF HE "RAN TV."

FIRST THING I'D DO IS CHANGE THE NAMES OF ALL THE TV NETWORKS.

abc — ANYTHING BUT COLOR

CBS — CAN'T BEAT SEGREGATION

NBC — NO BROWN CHARACTERS

FOX — FULL-ON XCLUSION

12/28
LALO ALCARAZ

©2002 LALO ALCARAZ /Dist. by Universal Press Syndicate

20

©2002 LALO ALCARAZ / Dist. by Universal Press Syndicate 12/29

CHUY'S DINER

YOU GOTTA LOVE MEXICAN BABY NEW YEAR...

MENUDO

JAN 01

SE FIA MAÑANA

FELIZ 2003

LALO ALCARAZ ©2002

21

EDDIE, I THINK OUR RELATIONSHIP IS IN TROUBLE.

WHY? I THINK IT'S PERFECT AS IT IS.

©2002 LALO ALCARAZ /Dist. by Universal Press Syndicate

PERFECT?

PERFECT.

AND YOU'RE WILLING TO SETTLE FOR THAT?

12/30

THANK YOU FOR COMING TO THE BOOKSTORE WITH ME, EDDIE. DOING ACTIVITIES WE BOTH ENJOY CAN KEEP OUR RELATIONSHIP FRESH.

NO PROBLEMO, VERO. I LOVE WHEN WE DO THINGS TOGETHER.

HOME DECOR BOOKS

©2002 LALO ALCARAZ /Dist. by Universal Press Syndicate

12/31

CAN WE LEAVE TOGETHER NOW?

RELATIONSHIP ADVICE BOOKS

©2003 LALO ALCARAZ /Dist. by Universal Press Syndicate

LET'S SEE... "MEN ARE FROM MEXICO, WOMEN ARE FROM VENEZUELA", "TORTILLA SOUP FOR THE SOUL"...

"J.LO'S GUIDE TO RELATIONSHIPS AND SERIAL MARRIAGE"

1/1

22

Panel 1: "HEY, GIRLFRIEND! JENNY FROM THE BLOCK HERE. IS YOUR RELATIONSHIP STAGNATING?"

J.LO's GUIDE TO RELATIONSHIPS + SERIAL MARRIAGE

©2003 LALO ALCARAZ /Dist. by Universal Press Syndicate

Panel 2: "MAYBE IT'S TIME TO REINVIGORATE YOUR RELATIONSHIP BY GETTING ENGAGED."

Panel 3: "BE SURE TO TELL YOUR CURRENT BOYFRIEND THAT YOU ARE GETTING ENGAGED TO SOMEONE ELSE."

LALO ALCARAZ 1/2

Panel 4: I'M NOT EAVESDROPPING, BUT IT SEEMS YOU HAVE A PROBLEM WITH COMMON "AMERICAN" SAYINGS...

Panel 5: OH WHAT? NOW YOU'RE GOING TO SAY IT'S BECAUSE I'M LATINO, AREN'T YOU?!

©2003 LALO ALCARAZ /Dist. by Universal Press Syndicate

LALO ALCARAZ 1/3

Panel 6: LIKE THEY SAY... "THOSE WHO LIVE IN GLASS HOUSES SHOULDN'T GET STONED."

Panel 7: MAYBE YOU'RE RIGHT... SOMETIMES WE CAN'T KEEP COMMON SAYINGS AND FIGURES OF SPEECH STRAIGHT...

Panel 8: I THINK IT MAKES US LOOK KIND OF STUPID...

©2003 LALO ALCARAZ /Dist. by Universal Press Syndicate

LALO ALCARAZ 1/4

Panel 9: WATCH IT, ROACHIE! YOU'RE SKATING ON HOT WATER!

23

IT'S A NEW YEAR! TIME TO RE-EVALUATE OUR LIVES AND SET NEW GOALS.

I'LL START. I COULD STAND TO BE A LITTLE LESS HOSTILE TO OTHERS...

EVEN IF THEY ARE COMPLETE MORONS.

FINE. I CAN BE A LITTLE PREACHY AT TIMES, SO I COULD CUT BACK ON LECTURING OTHERS ABOUT THEIR INCORRECT POLITICAL STANDS — EVEN WHILE MINE ARE ALWAYS RIGHT!

LALO ALCARAZ ©2003

1/5

I GUESS I CAN TRY TO PAY MORE ATTENTION IN SCHOOL.

MAYBE I CAN EVEN BUMP UP MY "C" IN SPANISH.

UH... I THINK I'M KIND OF GETTING A BEER GUT...

SO NO MORE TIGHT T-SHIRTS FOR ME!

24

Panel 1: EDDIE, HOMIE... I LEFT MY WALLET AT THE PAD. CAN YOU SPOT ME A TWENTY FOR THE DRINKS?

Panel 2: UH..., YEAH, OKAY. / COOL.

Panel 3: NOW TO FIND ME ANOTHER SUCKER TO PAY FOR DINNER! / I THINK YOU SHOULD HAVE USED A THOUGHT BUBBLE FOR THAT.

©2003 LALO ALCARAZ /Dist. by Universal Press Syndicate — 1/6

Panel 1: OH NO! **NO!** I THINK THEY DROPPED MY FAVORITE COMIC STRIP!!

Panel 2: WHAT'S YOUR FAVORITE COMIC STRIP, EDDIE? / UH... NEVER MIND, CUCO...

Panel 3: OKAY... "WHITESVILLE, U.S.A." / COME ON, IT'S A QUAINT, OLD-FASHIONED COMIC STRIP ABOUT THE "GOOD OL' DAYS."

Panel 4: YOU LIKE "WHITESVILLE, U.S.A."?! / OH YEAH, THE "GOOD OL' DAYS"— WHEN THERE WERE **NO** MINORITIES!?

©2003 LALO ALCARAZ /Dist. by Universal Press Syndicate — 1/7

Panel 1: **DEAR EDITOR,** I CANNOT BELIEVE YOU HAVE REPLACED MY FAVORITE EIGHTY-YEAR-OLD COMIC STRIP WITH "**LA CUCARACHA**".

Panel 2: "LA CUCARACHA" IS NOT ONLY DRAWN BY A HISPANIC, BUT IT ONLY FEATURES HISPANIC CHARACTERS – WHICH MAKES IT A TOTALLY RACIST COMIC STRIP!

Panel 3: PLEASE DROP "LA CUCARACHA" AND BRING BACK MY FAVORITE COMIC STRIP, "**WHITESVILLE, USA**" BY ARYAN McCRACKER.

©2003 LALO ALCARAZ /Dist. by Universal Press Syndicate — 1/8

Panel 1: I BET THIS GUY'S TACO CART IS RATED BY "ZAGAT."

Panel 2: OH SI, SEÑOR, THIS IS A FOUR-STAR ZAGAT-RATED SIDEWALK TACO CART. THE RESERVATIONS WAITING LIST IS SIX MONTHS LONG. WOULD YOU LIKE TO SEE A WINE LIST?

LALO ALCARAZ 1/9

Panel 3: GEE, I HOPE THE GREASE IS HALF AS THICK AS THE SARCASM.

WAIT, YOU'RE THE FOOD REVIEWER FROM GOURMET MAGAZINE, RIGHT?

©2003 LALO ALCARAZ /Dist. by Universal Press Syndicate

Panel 1: AND IT WAS... UH ER AH...

HIJOLE! SOMETIMES I WISH I WAS.., UH...

Panel 2: WHAT'S THAT WORD WHERE YOU SAY THE RIGHT WORD AT THE RIGHT TIME?!

1/10

Panel 3: "ARTICULATE"?

NO, THAT'S NOT IT.

©2003 LALO ALCARAZ /Dist. by Universal Press Syndicate

Panel 1: DID YOU HEAR THE RUMOR THAT BLONDES WERE SUPPOSED TO GO EXTINCT BY THE YEAR 2208?

Panel 2: REALLY? NO WONDER THEY'VE CREATED A BLONDE WILDLIFE PRESERVE TO SAVE THE SPECIES.

©2003 LALO ALCARAZ /Dist. by Universal Press Syndicate

Panel 3: 1/11 LALO ALCARAZ

REALLY? WHERE?

SPANISH LANGUAGE TV.

26

©2003 Lalo Alcaraz /Dist. por Universal Press Syndicate Y Que!

TAKE ME TO YOUR LEADER.

PSST PSST PSST PST

LALO ALCARAZ ©2003 DISTRIBUTED BY UNIVERSAL PRESS SYNDICATE

1/12

THOSE CREATURES DID NOT HAVE A LEADER?

NO. THEY ARE KNOWN AS "LATINOS."

27

Panel 1: A NEW SURVEY HAS FOUND THAT "LATINOS OVERWHELMINGLY EMBRACE THE ENGLISH LANGUAGE."

Panel 2: WOW! SUCH A STUNNING REVELATION! WHAT OTHER THINGS DID LATINOS SURPRISINGLY EMBRACE?

Panel 3: "BEANS... AND RICE"!

1/13 LALO ALCARAZ
©2003 LALO ALCARAZ /Dist. by Universal Press Syndicate

Panel 1: I DON'T UNDERSTAND WHY AMERICA DOESN'T GET THAT LATINO IMMIGRANTS ALL WANT TO LEARN ENGLISH.

Panel 2: LOOK, THERE GO TWO LATINOS SPEAKING IN SPANISH.

LALO ALCARAZ 1/14

Panel 3: IT'S LIKE NOBODY LISTENS TO EACH OTHER ANYMORE.

Panel 4: THEY'RE PROBABLY TALKING ABOUT ME RIGHT NOW.

©2003 LALO ALCARAZ /Dist. by Universal Press Syndicate

Panel 1: DID YOU HEAR ABOUT THIS? RON HOWARD WAS SET TO DIRECT A NEW FILM VERSION OF "THE ALAMO."

Panel 2: YOU MEAN "OPIE"? THE GUY WHO RECAST A REAL LATINA ROLE WITH AN ANGLO ACTRESS IN "A BEAUTIFUL MIND"?

LALO ALCARAZ 1/15
©2003 LALO ALCARAZ /Dist. by Universal Press Syndicate

Panel 3: NEVER MIND. IT SAYS HE LATER DROPPED OUT OF THE PROJECT.

Panel 4: HE WAS PROBABLY UPSET WHEN HE FOUND OUT THAT MEXICANS WON AT THE ALAMO!

28

OH, VERO... YOU HAVE THAT CERTAIN... OH! WHAT'S THAT FRENCH PHRASE!?

JE NE SAIS QUOI?

YO NO SE,

I DON'T KNOW,

HEY, CUCO, WHAT'S THAT?

I'M CREATING A PAINTING FOR CHEECH MARIN'S TOURING CHICANO ART EXHIBIT.

EN SERIO?! CHEECH ACTUALLY ASKED YOU FOR AN ART PIECE?

NOT EXACTLY, BUT HE'S GONNA LOVE IT! ONE FINAL TOUCH...

VOILÀ!

IT'S ON FIRE!

I CALL IT "UP IN SMOKE,"

WHAT WOULD JESUS (GONZALEZ) DRIVE?

A SLAMMED '47 CHEVY FLEETLINE,

29

HOMEMADE POPCORN? CHECK.

GIANT SODA? CHECK.

FRESH GUM ON CARPET? CHECK!

THIS MOVIE LOOKED HORRIBLE IN THE PREVIEWS, REMEMBER? OH YEAH...

ALL THE MOVIE REVIEWERS GAVE IT 1/2 STAR OR LESS!

BOB SMITH OF FICTITIOUS RADIO NETWORK SAID; "THIS FILM IS SO BAD I SENT MY BRIBE BACK!"

MY COUSIN RUDY SAID IT WAS THE BIGGEST STINKER SINCE "ENOUGH."

WOW! P.U.! ¡HÍJOLE!

THAT MOVIE MADE LESS MONEY THAN THE TEENAGERS WORKING AT THE THEATER!

IT LEFT THE THEATERS FASTER THAN HALLE BERRY AT AN ACCIDENT SCENE!

I'M GLAD THE DVD FINALLY CAME OUT! YEAH!

SHHHHH! IT'S STARTING!

1/19 LALO ALCARAZ

30

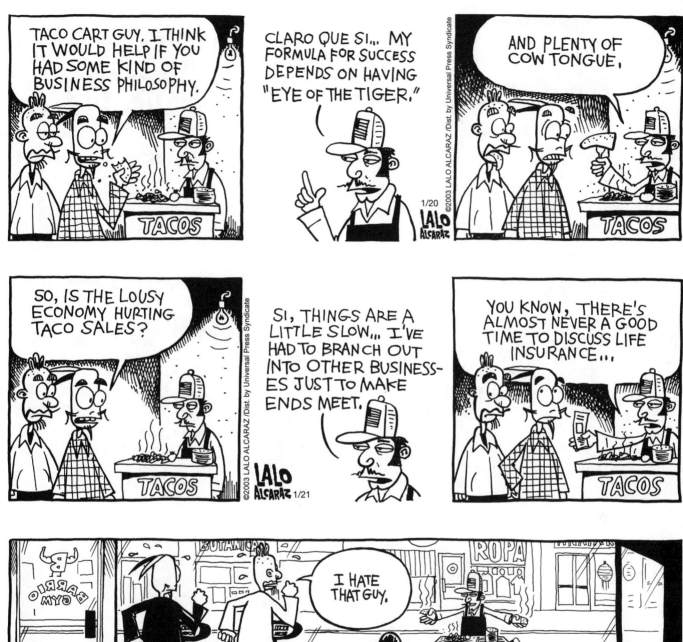

TACO CART GUY, I THINK IT WOULD HELP IF YOU HAD SOME KIND OF BUSINESS PHILOSOPHY.

CLARO QUE SI... MY FORMULA FOR SUCCESS DEPENDS ON HAVING "EYE OF THE TIGER,"

AND PLENTY OF COW TONGUE,

SO, IS THE LOUSY ECONOMY HURTING TACO SALES?

SI, THINGS ARE A LITTLE SLOW... I'VE HAD TO BRANCH OUT INTO OTHER BUSINESSES JUST TO MAKE ENDS MEET.

YOU KNOW, THERE'S ALMOST NEVER A GOOD TIME TO DISCUSS LIFE INSURANCE...

I HATE THAT GUY.

©2003 LALO ALCARAZ /Dist. by Universal Press Syndicate

31

Panel 1 (1/23): THEY'RE TRYING TO BRING BACK THE DRAFT?! / DID THE ARMY FINALLY RUN OUT OF POOR, EAGER LATINOS?!

Panel 2: THEY MUST HAVE RECRUITED EVERY LAST LATINO KID. / WHO COULD RESIST THEIR CATCHY NEW SLOGAN? / ☆AN ARMY OF JUAN / ARMY RECRUITMENT OFFICE / ENLIST / ©2003 LALO ALCARAZ /Dist. by Universal Press Syndicate

©2003 LALO ALCARAZ /Dist. by Universal Press Syndicate

Panel (1/24): ARMY RECRUITMENT / HOLA, YOUNG MAN! ARE YOU OVER 18?

Panel: YEAH, / HAVE YOU EVER CONSIDERED ENLISTING IN "AN ARMY OF JUAN"?

Panel: ARMY...TMENT / WHAT HE'S ASKING IS, "DO YOU JUAN TO DIE?"

Panel (1/25): ENLIST AND FIGHT OUR NATION'S ENEMIES! / ENEMY / ©2003 LALO ALCARAZ /Dist. by Universal Press Syndicate

32

©2003 Lalo Alcaraz / DIST. by Universal Press Syndicate

THESE LARGE DISCOUNT RETAILERS ARE KILLING US LITTLE GUYS.

TACO★MART

TACOS

Panel 1: HAVE A GOOD DAY AT WORK, VERO!

THANKS FOR DROPPING ME OFF AT SCHOOL, EDDIE.

SURE, GO FILL THEIR LITTLE BRAINS WITH WORTHLESS PROPAGANDA!

Panel 2: KNOCK IT OFF, CUCO! I KNOW I'M ONLY A TEACHING ASSISTANT... BUT I'M TRYING TO CHANGE THE SYSTEM FROM THE **INSIDE**!

1/27 ©2003 LALO ALCARAZ /Dist. by Universal Press Syndicate

Panel 3: PIONEER ELEMENTARY HOME OF THE "FIGHTIN' SAVAGES"

FROM THE OUTSIDE IN...

Panel 4: GOOD MORNING, MRS. RAMOS.

GOOD MORNING, VERONICA.

Panel 5: TODAY WE'RE TEACHING THE CHILDREN ABOUT THE GLORIOUS DISCOVERY OF AMERICA.

©2003 LALO ALCARAZ /Dist. by Universal Press Syndicate

Panel 6: I CAN REMEMBER WHEN FAIRY TALES WERE TOLD AT NIGHTTIME...

LALO ALCARAZ 1/28

Panel 7: JOSÉ, CHECK OUT THIS LUNCH BAG I JUST 'DISCOVERED"!

LALO ALCARAZ

Panel 8: HUH? **HEY!** THAT'S **MY** LUNCH! YOU CAN'T "DISCOVER" SOMETHING THAT'S ALREADY THERE AND BELONGS TO SOMEONE ELSE. AND CLAIM IT FOR YOUR OWN...

©2003 LALO ALCARAZ /Dist. by Universal Press Syndicate

Panel 9: WAIT A MINUTE— THAT'S NOT WHAT IT SAYS IN THIS BOOK.

NOW THAT'S "DISCOVERY."

COLUMBUS

1/29

34

VAMONOS, VERO, WE'RE GONNA GRAB BREAKFAST AT CHUY'S DINER.

WHAT?! THAT DIVE IS DIRTY AND HAS TERRIBLE SERVICE!

THE FOOD IS SUPER GREASY AND THE WAITRESS IS INSANE!

WHAT COULD YOU POSSIBLY LIKE ABOUT THAT?!

BIG PORTIONS OF ALL OF THE ABOVE!

CHUY'S DINER

©2003 LALO ALCARAZ /Dist. by Universal Press Syndicate

LALO ALCARAZ 1/30

¡BUENOS DIAS, CHUY! GIMME THE BREAKFAST PLATE, BUT CAN I GET FRIJOLES?

BEANS ARE EXTRA.

AND CORN TORTILLAS,

THAT'S EXTRA.

OVER-EASY EGGS,

EGGS ARE EXTRA.

WHAT'S **NOT** EXTRA?

THE PLATE.

GREAT! AT LEAST I DON'T HAVE TO PAY MORE FOR A CLEAN PLATE!

THAT'S EXTRA.

LALO ALCARAZ 1/31

©2003 LALO ALCARAZ /Dist. by Universal Press Syndicate

HEALTH INSPECTORS?

NO, U.N. WEAPONS INSPECTORS.

SE FIA MAÑANA

UN

CHILE

©2003 LALO ALCARAZ /Dist. by Universal Press Syndicate

LALO ALCARAZ 2/1

35

ART MUSEUM
CHEECH MARIN
TRAVELING CHICANO
ART EXHIBIT
"CHICANO VISIONS"
SPONSORED BY
◎ TARGET

COOL! WE'RE FINALLY HERE!

LET'S GET A SOUVENIR T-SHIRT FIRST!

NICE DREAMS ICE CREAM | MUNCHIES
SOUVENIRS

LALO 2/2 ALCARAZ

©2003 Lalo Alcaraz / DIST. by Universal Press Syndicate

ORALE! LET'S WALK IN AND SEE THE SHOW!

MAYBE WE SHOULD RUN IN...

CONVENTION CENTER
WELCOME ARIZONA BORDER VIGILANTES

CHEECH MARIN ART SHOW

CHEECH MARIN ART SHOW

36

Panel 1: IN ENTERTAINMENT NEWS... PRODUCERS OF "THE ALAMO" WERE DISTRESSED BECAUSE THEY COULD NOT FIND SKINNY MEXICAN-AMERICAN EXTRAS TO PLAY MEXICAN SOLDIERS.

Panel 2: ALSO IN SAN ANTONIO, TEXAS...

Panel 3: "LOS LOBOS" WERE BANNED FROM THE SET AFTER AUDITIONING TO PLAY THE HOUSE BAND AT THE ALAMO. 2/3

Panel 1: AND NOW IT'S TIME FOR THE HIP-HOP NEWS...

Panel 2: A NEW STUDY SAYS LATINOS ARE NOW THE MOST OVERWEIGHT ETHNIC GROUP IN THE U.S.A., ...

Panel 3: IN A RELATED STORY, LATINO RAPPER "FAT JOE" OPENED FOR EMINEM AND ATE HIM. 2/4

Panel 1: OH I **HATE** THIS SONG!

Panel 2: I KNOW, ME TOO! THE LYRICS ARE SOOO STUPID! IT'S **SO** PLAYED OUT! I HATE THIS "ACTRESS-SINGER," WHAT A NO-TALENT. 2/5

Panel 3: TURN IT UP. OKAY.

37

Strip 1 (2/6):

DID YOU KNOW IT HELPS TO HAVE A "WHITE" NAME?

¿QUE QUE?

RESEARCHERS SENT OUT JOB APPLICATIONS WITH "BLACK SOUNDING" NAMES vs. "WHITE SOUNDING" NAMES, AND THE WHITE-NAMED APPLICATIONS GOT **50%** MORE RESPONSES FROM EMPLOYERS.

I THINK WE SHOULD GET "WHITE" NAMES!

I'LL BE "DAVID DUKE" AND YOU BE "CARROT TOP"!

©2003 LALO ALCARAZ /Dist. by Universal Press Syndicate

Strip 2 (2/7):

THIS STUDY IS ACTUALLY ABOUT HOW EMPLOYERS GIVE PREFERENTIAL TREATMENT TO "WHITE SOUNDING" **FIRST NAMES.**

DO YOU REALLY THINK HAVING A "WHITE SOUNDING" FIRST NAME CAN GET YOU BETTER TREATMENT?

SURE IT CAN...

JUST ASK "BRETT BIN LADEN."

©2003 LALO ALCARAZ /Dist. by Universal Press Syndicate

Strip 3 (2/8):

©2003 LALO ALCARAZ /Dist. by Universal Press Syndicate

COOL SHIRT, DUDE.

THANKS.

HE WAS GREAT, TOTALLY MY HERO.

ME TOO.

WHAT A REBEL, HUH?

YEP.

SO WHERE CAN I GET A COOL JIM MORRISON SHIRT, TOO?

38

BARRIOBUCKS COFFEE AND CHECK CASHING

©2003 LALO ALCARAZ /Dist. by Universal Press Syndicate

TALL CINNAMON LATTÉ FOR ALICIA!

GRACIAS.

CUCO, DID YOU SEE THAT? HER COFFEE ORDER MATCHED HER TO A TEE!

GET OUT.

SHORT VANILLA CAPPUCCINO FOR MIKE!

THANKS!

DUDE. DID YOU SEE THAT?!

NO.

LALO ALCARAZ

2/9

I THINK I'VE DISCOVERED A NEW THEORY!

TRIPLE GRANDE CHOCOLATE MOCHA FOR OSO!

OKAY, CHICANO EINSTEIN, I'M GOING TO ORDER YOU A DRINK THAT WILL MATCH YOU PERFECTLY...

COOL!

EXCUSE ME, WHAT IS YOUR LAMEST COFFEE DRINK?

DECAF.

39

Panel 1: SORRY, VERO, **J.LO** IS JUST NOT A GOOD SINGER. / SHE IS TOO!

Panel 2: J.LO IS GIVING TRULY TALENTED LATIN SINGERS A BAD NAME. 2/10

Panel 3: OH YEAH? LIKE WHO? / OSCAR DE LA HOYA.

Panel 4: DO YOU KNOW WHY I PULLED YOU OVER? / ACTUALLY, YES, OFFICER. A RECENT NATIONWIDE FLURRY OF STATISTICAL STUDIES AND REPORTS INDICATES MOTORISTS OF COLOR ARE STOPPED BY POLICE IN GREATER PERCENTAGES THAN THEIR NUMBERS IN THE POPULATION.

Panel 5: CAN I REMEMBER JUST ONCE TO STOP ASKING RHETORICAL QUESTIONS!? / DO YOU MIND? I WASN'T DONE YET! 2/11

Panel 6: WOULD YOU PLEASE / GET OUT OF THE CAR? / IT'S FUNNY YOU ASK THAT, RECENT STUDIES HAVE SHOWN THAT AFTER BEING PULLED OVER BY POLICE, PEOPLE OF COLOR WERE MORE LIKELY TO BE ASKED TO EXIT THEIR VEHICLES THAN WHITE MOTORISTS.

Panel 7: WOULD YOU PLEASE TURN OFF YOUR HAZARD BLINKERS? / AND HAVE A NICE DAY! 2/12

40

©2003 LALO ALCARAZ /Dist. by Universal Press Syndicate

LALO ALCARAZ 2/13

I LIKE THAT BUSH HOMBRE. HE'S A GUY'S GUY!

HE'S JUST NOT FOR THE LITTLE GUY, THE POOR GUY, THE BLACK GUY, THE BROWN GUY, THE WOMAN GUY...

©2003 LALO ALCARAZ /Dist. by Universal Press Syndicate

LALO ALCARAZ 2/14

YOU ARE JUST A WHINER, AMIGO. AMERICA IS A GREAT LAND OF OPPORTUNITY!

NOBODY NEEDS THINGS LIKE "AFFIRMATIVE ACTION."

WHAT?

AMERICA IS A "MERITOCRACY."

YES, YOU ARE JUDGED SOLELY ON THE MERITS OF YOUR CONNECTIONS.

©2003 LALO ALCARAZ /Dist. by Universal Press Syndicate

LALO ALCARAZ 2/15

CUCO! STOP BUGGING THIS GUY! SORRY ABOUT MY FRIEND, SEÑOR.

IT'S OKAY, JOVEN. I'M USED TO IT.

AS A STAUNCH REPUBLICAN RANCHERO, I HAVE PLENTY OF DETRACTORS.

WELL, I HOPE NO MORE DETRACTORS SHOW UP HERE.

DON'T BE SILLY. I KEEP DETRACTORS ON DE FARM.

41

ARE YOU COUNTERFEITING MONEY AGAIN, CUCO?!

CHILL OUT, EDDIE. I'M JUST SUBMITTING PROPOSED REDESIGNS FOR THE NEW U.S. CURRENCY.

THE GOVERNMENT SAID THEY'RE FINALLY ADDING SOME COLOR TO OUR BILLS.

NOW AVAILABLE IN COLOR

DOLORES HUERTA

GERONIMO

MALCOLM X

MLK JR.

CESAR CHAVEZ

"AT 37 MILLION, PEOPLE WHO IDENTIFY THEMSELVES AS 'LATINO' ARE NOW THE LARGEST MINORITY IN THE UNITED STATES."

AT THIS RATE, THE U.S. WILL BE TOTALLY LATINO BY 2004...

...IF YOU ADD IN LATINOS WHO THINK THEY'RE WHITE, LATINOS WHO DON'T KNOW WHAT THEY ARE, WHITE PEOPLE WHO GO SALSA DANCING...

LATINOS ARE NOW THE BIGGEST MINORITY... WHICH BRINGS ME TO MY NEXT OBSERVATION—

NOT A PEEP OUT OF YOU, DUDE.

McTACO

THAT WAS A GREAT TV SHOW LAST NIGHT.

I DIDN'T THINK I'D LIKE IT, BUT IT WAS ACTUALLY PRETTY COOL...

THE DRAMA OF RUNNING A CRIME ENTERPRISE AND DEALING WITH YOUR ETHNIC FAMILY WAS, LIKE ... DRAMATIC!

VIOLENCE, DRUGS AND BRUTALITY! MAN, I LOVE "THE SOPRANOS"!

NO, NOT "THE SOPRANOS," WE'RE TALKING ABOUT "KINGPIN," A CRIME SHOW ABOUT LATINOS.

THEN WE MUST PROTEST!

43

LALO ALCARAZ 2/20

I'VE GOT A PILE OF WORK TO DO... WHAT'S THE BEST WAY TO APPROACH IT?

CHECK MY E-MAIL!

-BEEP-

Eddie, Hey cousin, it's Chava. We shipped out last week and we're now on the ground near the Gulf.

I really miss home, esp. the food. On a serious note, my life may be in danger...

...if the guys find out I've been hoarding the canned tortillas my mom sent me.

©2003 LALO ALCARAZ /Dist. by Universal Press Syndicate

Hey cousin Chava, it's good to hear from you. I hope you're safe in the desert.

2/21

Dear primo, I can't say exactly where I'm at because of security reasons.

Let's just say, compared to my old neighborhood...

...this place may not have as many weapons.

LALO ALCARAZ

©2003 LALO ALCARAZ /Dist. by Universal Press Syndicate

MEANWHILE, IN IRAQ...

USA SANCHEZ   USA LOPEZ

COMMANDER, I MIGHT BE SEEING THINGS, BUT IT SEEMS WE ARE ABOUT TO BE INVADED BY THE COMBINED ARMIES OF MEXICO AND PUERTO RICO.

2/22

LALO ALCARAZ

©2003 LALO ALCARAZ /Dist. by Universal Press Syndicate

44

WHAT'S THE DATE TODAY, CUCO?

LET ME SEE...

LALO ALCARAZ 2/23

WAIT A MINUTE... YOU'RE GOING TO TELL ME THE DATE BY READING THE AZTEC CALENDAR?!

EDDIE, YOU'RE SO WOEFULLY IGNORANT OF YOUR OWN HISTORY. THE AZTEC CALENDAR, OR SUN STONE, ALSO KNOWN AS CUAHXICALLI (EAGLE BOWL), WAS CARVED AND DEDICATED IN 1479 FOR THE AZTEC RULER AXAYACATL IN HONOR OF THEIR PRINCIPAL DEITY, THE SUN.

THE AZTECS, OR MEXICA, COUNTED TIME TWO WAYS, THE TONALPOHUALLI, A 260-DAY CYCLE, AND THE XIUHPOHUALLI, A 365-DAY SOLAR COUNT.

THE 260-DAY CYCLE OF THE TONALPOHUALLI WAS ORGANIZED INTO 20 DAYS, EACH OF WHICH WAS ASSIGNED A CERTAIN PATRON, HIEROGLYPH AND NUMBER. THE 20 NAMED DAYS CORRESPOND WITH THE NUMBERS 1 TO 13, FORMING NEW COMBINATIONS OF DAY NAMES.

EACH 260-DAY CYCLE IS COMPOSED OF 20 WEEKS OF 13 DAYS. THE TONALPOHUALLI IS FURTHER DIVISIBLE BY 2, 4 AND 5. DIVIDING BY 5 GIVES US 52 DAYS, 52 YEARS BEING THE AZTEC CENTURY.

SO WHAT'S THE DATE?!

THE 23RD.

©2003 LALO ALCARAZ /Dist. by Universal Press Syndicate

45

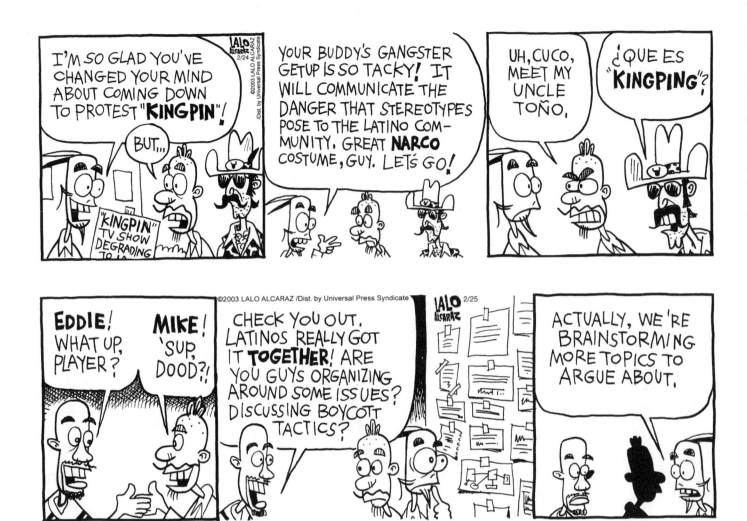

Panel 1: I'M SO GLAD YOU'VE CHANGED YOUR MIND ABOUT COMING DOWN TO PROTEST "KINGPIN"! — BUT... — "KINGPIN" TV SHOW DEGRADING TO LA...

LALO ALCARAZ 2/24 ©2003 LALO ALCARAZ /Dist. by Universal Press Syndicate

Panel 2: YOUR BUDDY'S GANGSTER GETUP IS SO TACKY! IT WILL COMMUNICATE THE DANGER THAT STEREOTYPES POSE TO THE LATINO COMMUNITY. GREAT NARCO COSTUME, GUY. LET'S GO!

Panel 3: UH, CUCO, MEET MY UNCLE TOÑO, — ¿QUE ES "KINGPING"?

©2003 LALO ALCARAZ /Dist. by Universal Press Syndicate — LALO ALCARAZ 2/25

Panel 4: EDDIE! WHAT UP, PLAYER? — MIKE! 'SUP, DOOD?!

Panel 5: CHECK YOU OUT, LATINOS REALLY GOT IT TOGETHER! ARE YOU GUYS ORGANIZING AROUND SOME ISSUES? DISCUSSING BOYCOTT TACTICS?

Panel 6: ACTUALLY, WE'RE BRAINSTORMING MORE TOPICS TO ARGUE ABOUT,

LALO ALCARAZ 2/26 — ©2003 LALO ALCARAZ /Dist. by Universal Press Syndicate

Panel 7: YOU'RE KIDDING ME, RIGHT? I ALWAYS THOUGHT LATINOS WERE TOGETHER, UNLIKE BLACK FOLK! — ¡VIVA ZAPATA!

Panel 8: WHAT?! I ALWAYS THOUGHT BLACKS HAD IT TOGETHER, UNLIKE LATINOS!

Panel 9: WOW... MAYBE BLACKS AND LATINOS SHOULD GET TOGETHER AND JOIN FORCES!

Panel 10: NAH!

46

SUGARY BLAMMO PUFFS?! YOU SURE DO EAT LIKE A LITTLE BABY!

CRUNCH HMMPHH SLURP

HOW'S YOUR KIDDIE CEREAL, "BABY"?

ALL RIGHT ALREADY! I'LL EAT SOME FIBER FLAKES, HIJOLE!

OH, BABY!

©2003 LALO ALCARAZ /Dist. by Universal Press Syndicate

LALO ALCARAZ 2/27

BRO... I HATE TO BRING THIS UP, BUT YOU'RE EATING ALL THE FOOD IN THE APARTMENT.

HMMMPH?

I THOUGHT WE AGREED TO SHARE THE FOOD COSTS. THAT IMPLIES WE SHARE THE **FOOD** TOO!

EDDIE, I'M A COCKROACH. "VORACIOUS" IS MY MIDDLE NAME!

DANG! I THOUGHT YOU SAID IT WAS "HORATIO."

©2003 LALO ALCARAZ /Dist. by Universal Press Syndicate

LALO ALCARAZ 2/28

WHERE ARE **YOU** RUSHING OFF TO?

©2003 LALO ALCARAZ /Dist. by Universal Press Syndicate

LALO ALCARAZ 3/1

I'M LATE FOR MY **LATINO TIME MANAGEMENT SEMINAR!**

47

I GET IT, I GET IT... SOMEONE'S A LITTLE TOO EXCITED ABOUT "MATRIX 2" COMING OUT THIS YEAR!

LALO ALCARAZ

©2003 LALO ALCARAZ /Dist. by Universal Press Syndicate

3/2

DO WE GET CESAR CHAVEZ DAY OFF THIS YEAR?

CUCO, WHAT ARE YOU TALKING ABOUT? YOU DON'T HAVE A JOB!

I PREFER TO SAY THAT I AM "BETWEEN HOLIDAYS."

©2003 LALO ALCARAZ /Dist. by Universal Press Syndicate

3/3

I DON'T REALLY GET THAT MANY HOLIDAYS OFF BECAUSE I WORK HERE AT THE "BARRIO BUGLE."

A STAFFER AT A TOP INVESTIGATIVE PUBLICATION LIKE THE "BARRIO BUGLE" CAN'T AFFORD TO TAKE A DAY OFF.

BE SERIOUS. WHAT'S THE LAST THING YOU INVESTIGATED?

THE WANT ADS.

©2003 LALO ALCARAZ /Dist. by Universal Press Syndicate

3/4

DANG! I'VE GOT A REALLY BAD COLD.

EDDIE, GET SOME LEMON JUICE, HONEY, CHOPPED JALAPEÑOS, ICE, POUR PLENTY OF TEQUILA OVER IT. NOW BLEND IT.

SO WHAT KIND OF COLD REMEDY IS THIS?

COLD REMEDY?

©2003 LALO ALCARAZ /Dist. by Universal Press Syndicate

3/5

49

VERO, BABE, I GOT YOU A GIFT.

PERFUME! OH, THANK YOU, EDDIE!

"THAT OLD LOWRIDER SMELL"?

I ALMOST GOT YOU "THAT NEW CAR SMELL", BUT I THOUGHT, "HOW IMPERSONAL."

©2003 LALO ALCARAZ /Dist. by Universal Press Syndicate

3/6

DID YOU HEAR THE NEWS?

THE PRESIDENT SAYS THAT THE OIL OF IRAQ BELONGS TO THE PEOPLE OF IRAQ AND WILL BE HELD IN A POST-WAR TRUST FOR THEM BY THE U.S. GOVERNMENT...

A TRUST MUCH LIKE THE INDIAN LAND TRUST!

HEY, WHAT'S THAT NOISE!?

I THINK IT'S LAUGHTER FROM THE RESERVATION.

©2003 LALO ALCARAZ /Dist. by Universal Press Syndicate

3/7

IF TV SHOWS WERE LIKE LATINO POLITICAL COMIC STRIPS...

OOOH! I HATE THIS SHOW!

HONEY, JUST CHANGE THE CHANNEL.

ABSOLUTELY NOT. I'M GOING DOWN TO THE TV STATION AND DEMAND THE SHOW BE YANKED SO NO ONE ELSE CAN SEE IT EITHER!

BUT UNTIL THEN, I WILL WATCH IT RELIGIOUSLY...

©2003 LALO ALCARAZ /Dist. by Universal Press Syndicate

3/8

50

APOLOGIES TO SCHULZ

LALO ALCARAZ
3/9

©2003 LALO ALCARAZ /Dist. by Universal Press Syndicate

PSYCHIATRIC HELP 5¢

THE DOCTOR IS IN

PSYCHIATRIC HELP 2¢

THE CHEAP IMMIGRANT LABOR IS IN

IT'S A CRAZY NEW WORLD, HOMES...

Panel 1 (3/10): EDDIE, REMEMBER WE'RE GOING TO MY COUSIN MARISELA'S LITTLE GIRL'S BAPTISM THIS SATURDAY AFTER WE GO TO THE...

Panel 2: COMMANDER LOPEZ, DO YOU COPY? OVER? COMMANDER?

Panel 3: SOMETIMES I FEEL LIKE YOU'RE TOTALLY NOT LISTENING TO ME! / YOU LOOK REALLY GOOD IN BLACK. / THANKS, BUT WE'RE NOT TALKING ABOUT THAT!

Panel 4 (3/11): YOU WERE THINKING ABOUT SOMETHING ELSE WHEN I WAS TALKING TO YOU... / EDDIE?

Panel 5: OH COMMANDER LOPEZ?...

Panel 6: YES, SPACE BABE ZEELTAR SIX? / KNOCK THAT OFF!

Panel 7 (3/12): SO WHAT WERE YOU THINKING ABOUT WHEN I WAS TALKING TO YOU?! / YOU DON'T WANT TO KNOW, VERO... / YES I DO!

Panel 9: ¿QUE PASO? OH NO, WERE YOU TOTALLY HONEST WITH VERO AGAIN? / HMTBR.

LALO ALCARAZ

©2003 LALO ALCARAZ /Dist. by Universal Press Syndicate

52

LALO ALCARAZ 3/13

BEER — DRINK BEER — BEER — AND MORE BEER

CERVEZA — TOMA CERVEZA — CERVEZA — Y MAS CERVEZA

THINGS ARE SO DIFFERENT SINCE THE LATINO MARKETING BOOM HIT.

©2003 LALO ALCARAZ /Dist. by Universal Press Syndicate

I'M BILL O'REILLY! WELCOME TO THE NO SPIN ZONE! THIS IS "THE O'REILLY FACTOR"!!

MY FIRST GUEST IS AN ADVOCATE FOR WETBACKS, er uh, I MEAN, ILLEGAL IMMIGRANTS.

BUT LET'S WET BACK— I MEAN, GET BACK TO HIM AFTER A WORD FROM OUR SPONSOR...

LALO ALCARAZ 3/14

WETBACK RESTAURANTS— I MEAN OUTBACK!

©2003 LALO ALCARAZ /Dist. by Universal Press Syndicate

I MISS THE OLD DAYS BEFORE TERROR ALERTS.

TERROR ALERT

DO YOU REMEMBER THOSE DAYS? THERE WASN'T ANY TERRORISM...

SURE, WE HAD TERRORISM...

WE JUST CALLED IT "GANG VIOLENCE."

©2003 LALO ALCARAZ /Dist. by Universal Press Syndicate

LALO ALCARAZ 3/15

53

THANK YOU FOR JOINING ME AT THIS GATHERING TO DISCUSS THE OUTRAGEOUS COMMERCIALIZATION OF **CINCO DE MAYO.**

COMMITTEE 5 DE MAYO

LALO ALCARAZ 3/16

©2003 LALO ALCARAZ /Dist. by Universal Press Syndicate

AN ETHNIC HOLIDAY MUST NEVER BECOME JUST ANOTHER ADVERTISING CAMPAIGN FOR ALCOHOL COMPANIES!

WE MUST REFUSE TO BECOME PAWNS IN THIS GAME OF MARKETING!

IF YOU'RE WITH ME, RAISE YOUR HANDS UP HIGH!

HAPPY St. Patrick's Day

54

Panel 1: OKAY, BYE,

Panel 2: SOMEBODY JUST STOLE MY IDENTITY.

©2003 LALO ALCARAZ /Dist. by Universal Press Syndicate 3/17

Panel 3: WAS THAT THE COPS ON THE PHONE?

Panel 4: NO, IT WAS THE IDENTITY THIEF BEGGING ME TO TAKE IT BACK,

Panel 1: SPANISH LANGUAGE ROCK IS SOOOOO COOL... I OUGHT TO START MY **OWN** "ROC EN ESPAÑOL" BAND.

Panel 2: LET'S SEE... I WOULD NEED A LEAD GUITARIST, A BASSIST, A DRUMMER...

Panel 3: AND SOMEONE WHO SPEAKS SPANISH.

©2003 LALO ALCARAZ /Dist. by Universal Press Syndicate 3/18

Panel 1: HOW CAN I WRITE A "ROC EN ESPAÑOL" SONG IF I CAN'T SPEAK SPANISH?

Panel 2: I KNOW... I'LL WRITE IT FIRST IN ENGLISH, THEN I'LL TRANSLATE IT INTO SPANISH.

Panel 3: **ENGLISH** "OH BABY BABY BABY."

Panel 4: **SPANISH** "O BEYBY BEYBY BEYBY."

©2003 LALO ALCARAZ /Dist. by Universal Press Syndicate 3/19

55

I DON'T KNOW WHAT MY ROC EN ESPAÑOL SONGS ARE GOING TO BE ABOUT!

YOU MUST WRITE A HEAVY RANT DECRYING OPPRESSION!

WRITE A TENDER BALLAD ABOUT RELATIONSHIPS...

A SONG ABOUT PARTYING WOULD BE SO **COOL!**

I WONDER WHAT'S SPANISH FOR "SURROUNDED BY KNUCKLEHEADS"?

©2003 LALO ALCARAZ /Dist. by Universal Press Syndicate
3/20

©2003 LALO ALCARAZ /Dist. by Universal Press Syndicate

CHUY'S DINER

HELLO, SIR, WOULD YOU BE INTERESTED IN PURCHASING SOME FINE PLASTIC MERCHANDISE?

DUDE, I'M TRYING TO HAVE MY LUNCH HERE. DO YOU MIND?

I WON'T BOTHER SHOWING YOU THE ELECTRIC EARWAX SCOOPER THEN.

3/21

THESE RUDE SOLICITORS. THEY'RE ALWAYS TRYING TO SELL FOOLS JUNK!

HEY, EDDIE, YOU WOULDN'T BELIEVE THIS PUSHY GUY TRYING TO SELL ME SOME STUFF WHILE I ATE!

REALLY? HEY, CAN YOU SPOT ME FIVE BUCKS FOR LUNCH? I JUST SPENT ALL MY MONEY.

3/22
©2003 LALO ALCARAZ /Dist. by Universal Press Syndicate

56

©2003 LALO ALCARAZ /Dist. by Universal Press Syndicate

LALO ALCARAZ 3/23

NETO, TIO TOÑO WANTS TO TALK TO YOU...

YOU MEAN LECTURE TO ME.

HI, UNCLE TOÑO.

HOLA, MIJO.

YOUR TIA CHELA AND I NEED A WORD WITH YOU.

YOUR STYLE OF CLOTHING IS BRINGING SHAME TO OUR FAMILY.

57

Panel 1: I THINK I JUST TUNED IN TO THAT NEW LIBERAL TALK RADIO NETWORK.

Panel 2: OH YEAH? HOW CAN YOU TELL?

Panel 3: NOTHING BUT WHITE PEOPLE ON IT. 3/24

Panel 1: YOU ARE LISTENING TO THE LIBERAL TALK RADIO NETWORK. I'M BARBRA STREISAND. AND I'M ED BEGLEY JR.

Panel 2: IT'S THE **BABS AND EDDIE MORNING ZOO!** WE'RE THE ANTIDOTE TO RIGHT-WING TALK RADIO...

Panel 3: WE PROMISE NEVER TO OFFEND OR BELITTLE ANYONE, OR HURT ANYONE'S FEELINGS...OR ENTERTAIN! NO SIR, NO ENTERTAINMENT HERE! 3/25

Panel 1: I JUST DON'T BUY BEN AFFLECK AS A SUPERHERO. DARE DEVIL IN THEATERS NOW 98¢ AND ABOVE

Panel 2: WHY NOT? WHAT'S HIS SUPERPOWER ANYWAY?

Panel 3: HIS GIANT HEAD IS THE ONLY THING THAT MAKES J.LO'S REAR END LOOK SMALLER. 3/26

58

Panel 1: I'M SO MAD ABOUT ALL THIS WAR TALK!

Panel 2: THAT'S IT. I'M WEARING MY **PEACE BUTTON** TO WORK.

Panel 3: ARE YOU ALLOWED TO DO THAT? IT **IS** A PUBLIC SCHOOL...

Panel 4: WE'RE SUPPOSED TO BE TEACHING KIDS TO THINK FOR THEMSELVES... SO WHY DO I HAVE TO STOP THINKING FOR MYSELF?

3/27

Panel 5: TEACHER VERONICA, IS THAT A "PEACE" BUTTON YOU'RE WEARING?

Panel 6: YES, PRINCIPAL MENDEZ, IT'S MY STATEMENT AGAINST WAR.

Panel 7: MAY I REMIND YOU, THIS IS A SCHOOL, NOT A PLACE FOR POLITICAL STATEMENTS. WE SHOULD APPEAR NEUTRAL TO THE STUDENTS.

Panel 8: HERE, COVER YOUR BUTTON WITH THIS "**GOD BLESS THE G.O.P.**" STICKER.

3/28

Panel 9: THE HISTORY OF AFFIRMATIVE ACTION: THE MOVIE

OKAY, I GOT THE PART ABOUT HOW AFFIRMATIVE ACTION EXISTED FOR OVER 200 YEARS FOR THE PRIVILEGED CLASS...

YEAH, BUT THEY LOST ME AT THE SURPRISE TWIST ENDING, WHEN THEY KILL IT AS SOON AS PEOPLE OF COLOR NEED IT.

I THOUGHT YOU SAID THIS WAS GONNA BE AN ACTION MOVIE!

3/29

59

LALO ALCARAZ 3/30

PIONEER ELEMENTARY "SCHOOL IS COOL" (APRIL FOOL!)

TEACHER VERONICA?

SINCE CESAR CHAVEZ WAS A GREAT HERO, WHEN DO YOU THINK THERE WILL BE A NATIONAL CESAR CHAVEZ HOLIDAY?

WELL, JOSÉ, WHEN ALL AMERICAN CONSUMERS DECIDE TO WAKE UP AT 4 A.M. AND GO TO THE FIELDS...

AND PICK VEGETABLE AND FRUIT CROPS IN THE FREEZING COLD AND THE BLAZING SUN...

WHILE BEING SPRAYED WITH TOXIC PESTICIDES...

©2003 LALO ALCARAZ /Dist. by Universal Press Syndicate

ONLY TO RETURN TO REST IN THEIR RAMSHACKLE, SUBSTANDARD HOUSING...

WHERE THEIR MEAGER PAYCHECKS AWAIT...

YOU COULD HAVE JUST SAID "NOT IN A MILLION YEARS!"

60

WELCOME TO OUR PUBLIC AFFAIRS PROGRAM...

THIS MORNING WE WILL DISCUSS THE LIBERAL MEDIA AND HOW IT HAS FOSTERED DIVERSITY IN AMERICA.

YOU ARE WATCHING ANOTHER EDITION OF "FIVE OLD WHITE GUYS DEBATE THE ISSUES."

HOLA, AMIGOS. MY NAME IS HOLA KITTY!

IT'S SO FUN BEING A PASSIVE HISPANIC KITTY! OLE!

LET'S PLAY "IMMIGRANT"! I'LL WORK CHEAP FOR YOU, THEN YOU CAN COMPLAIN ABOUT IT!

MI NOMBRE ES "HOLA KITTY"!

BUT I WON'T SPEAK SPANISH IF IT OFFENDS YOUR IGNORANT, NARROW-MINDED EARS!

SO THAT'S YOUR NEW COMIC STRIP? IT'S UH... CUTE, BUT DISTURBING. LIKE, YOU HAVE UTTER DISGUST FOR SOCIETY.

HMM... SO THE SUBTLE APPROACH ISN'T WORKING.

LALO ALCARAZ 3/31

4/1

4/2

61

Panel 1: CUCO, DID YOU KNOW THE **INS** HAS BEEN SHUT DOWN?

WHAT?! YOU MEAN ALL THOSE YEARS OF LETTER WRITING PAID OFF?!

Panel 2: AND YOU SAID MY "SOMBRERO-WEARING CALVIN DISSIN' ON THE MIGRA" STICKER MANUFACTURING WAS HOPELESS!

LALO ALCARAZ 4/3

MIGRA

Panel 3: I WOULDN'T EXACTLY BE THROWING AN "OPEN BORDERS" PARTY RIGHT AWAY...

OMIGOD! WHAT AM I GONNA DO WITH ALL THESE STUPID STICKERS?!

Panel 1: IT'S MORE LIKE A GOOD NEWS, BAD NEWS SITUATION.

HOW SO?

Panel 2: THE GOOD NEWS IS THAT THE **INS** HAS BEEN PUT OUT OF BUSINESS.

Panel 3: THE BAD NEWS IS THAT IT'S BEEN ABSORBED INTO THE NEW "BUREAU OF HARASSING ARABS AND LATINOS THAT JUST LOOK ARAB."

4/4 LALO ALCARAZ

Panel 1: I THINK IT'S A DISGRACE HOW LATINOS DIDN'T SUPPORT THE **ESTRADA** JUDICIAL NOMINATION.

YOU'RE RIGHT! HE'S A LATINO ROLE MODEL. HE'S DONE A LOT FOR OUR VISIBILITY!

Panel 2: HIS WORK IN LAW ENFORCEMENT AND TRAFFIC REGULATION OUGHT TO BE ENOUGH REASON TO APPROVE HIM FOR THE HIGH COURT!

4/5 LALO ALCARAZ

Panel 3: I SAY MAKE **ERIK ESTRADA** HEAD OF HOMELAND SECURITY, TOO!

THE GUY'S NAME IS **MIGUEL** ESTRADA.

WHO THE HECK IS THAT?!

62

NOW THAT YOU DRAGGED ME DOWN HERE, ARE YOU GOING TO TELL ME HOW THIS SPORT IS REACHING OUT TO LATINOS?

ONE WORD: MONSTER TACO TRUCKS!

DID I JUST CALL MONSTER TRUCK RALLY A "SPORT"?

SUNDAY! SUNDAY! SUNDAY! MONSTER TRUCK RALLY

TACOZILLA

BONDO BURGERS

REFRIED MOTOR OIL

PELON'S UPHOLSTERY

SPECIAL THANKS TO MR. KEVANY'S 7th GRADE ENGLISH/ HISTORY CLASS AT IRVING MIDDLE SCHOOL!

©2003 LALO ALCARAZ /Dist. by Universal Press Syndicate 4/6

63

WOULD YOU LIKE TO TRY OUR NEW ITEM?

IT'S THE "DIET TACO."

IT'S A TORTILLA CHIP...

WHAT'S WRONG, CHUY? SOMETHING ON YOUR MIND?

MY GRANDSON IS IN THE GULF RIGHT NOW, AND I JUST CAN'T CONCENTRATE ON ANYTHING...

HOW COULD YOU TELL?

FOR STARTERS, YOU GOT MY ORDER RIGHT,

AND MINE'S EDIBLE!

DON'T WORRY, CHUY. YOUR GRANDSON WILL BE OKAY IN THE GULF, OUR BOYS WILL COME HOME SOON!

OH THANK YOU, CUCO, I THINK I'LL BE OKAY...

CHECK YOU OUT, MR. PATRIOT!

HEY! MILITANT PEACE-MONGERS HAVE FEELINGS TOO...

64

Panel 1: HOW IS YOUR CLASS-WORK GOING, JOSÉ? — GOOD, PRINCIPAL MENDEZ! TODAY WE LEARNED ABOUT DISSENTERS!

Panel 2: WHAT? — AND THEIR PEACE SIGNS ARE SO COOL!

Panel 3: WHAT ARE YOU TEACHING THIS CHILD, TEACHER VERONICA?! — DECLARATION OF INDEPENDENCE UNIT, WHY?

LALO ALCARAZ 4/10 ©2003 LALO ALCARAZ /Dist. by Universal Press Syndicate

Panel 1: DID YOU HEAR THE ONE ABOUT J. LO AND THE SOFA AND— — I SWEAR, IF I HEAR YOU TWO CRACK ONE MORE **J. LO** JOKE I'M GOING TO SCREAM LIKE A WOUNDED BEAST!

Panel 2: OR YOU COULD JUST PLAY HER LATEST ALBUM TO MUCH THE SAME EFFECT.

LALO ALCARAZ 4/11 ©2003 LALO ALCARAZ /Dist. by Universal Press Syndicate

Panel 1: I WANNA SEE THAT CHRIS ROCK MOVIE ABOUT THE FIRST BLACK PRESIDENT. — YEAH, ME TOO!

Panel 2: DO YOU THINK WE'LL EVER SEE A MEXICAN PRESIDENT?

Panel 3: SURE, WHEN WE GO TO MEXICO CITY.

LALO ALCARAZ 4/12 ©2003 LALO ALCARAZ /Dist. by Universal Press Syndicate

65

WHY ARE THERE SO FEW LATINO FILMS?

AND WHY DO THEY MOSTLY STINK?

DUMB DEVIL
REALLY OLD SCHOOL
HOW TO LOSE A GUY IN 90 MINUTES
GANGS OF D.C.

MAYBE LATINOS SHOULD LOOK TO AFRICAN-AMERICAN CINEMA FOR INSPIRATION...

I CAN SEE IT NOW...

"A COMEDY SET IN A SAN FRANCISCO NEIGHBORHOOD TAQUERIA THAT'S THE CENTER OF SOCIAL LIFE, FROM THE CREATORS OF BARBERSHOP, IT'S..."

WHAT DO YOU MEAN "THERE'S TOO MANY IMMIGRANTS"?!

IF WE CAN'T TALK STRAIGHT IN A TACO STAND, WHERE CAN WE?!

BURRITOSHOP

OR "AN UPTIGHT LATINA TRAVELS TO ACAPULCO AND FALLS FOR A MUY GUAPO CLIFF DIVER/CUMBIA INSTRUCTOR..."

HOW CONSUELO GOT HER GROOVE BACK

"FROM THE DIRECTOR OF FRIDAY AND THE HAIRDRESSER OF FRIDA COMES AN ART-HOUSE GHETTO COMEDY SEQUEL..."

THAT EYEBROW IS ILL!

Next Frida

THOSE IDEAS ARE CONTRIVED, DERIVATIVE AND LAME!

YOU'RE RIGHT. WE SHOULD GET AGENTS!

©2003 LALO ALCARAZ /Dist. by Universal Press Syndicate

4/13 LALO ALCARAZ

66

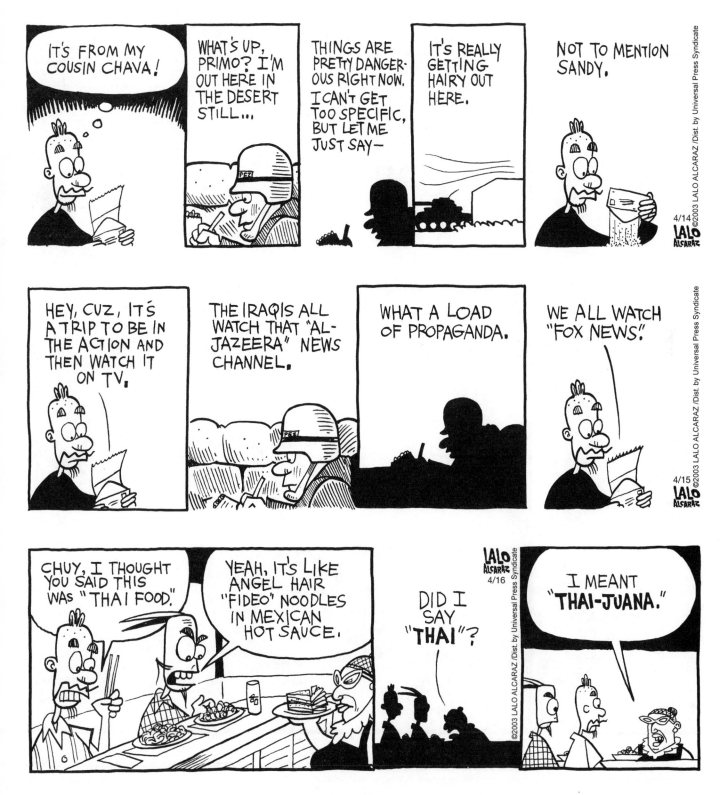

It's from my cousin Chava!

What's up, primo? I'm out here in the desert still...

Things are pretty dangerous right now. I can't get too specific, but let me just say—

It's really getting hairy out here.

Not to mention Sandy.

4/14 ©2003 LALO ALCARAZ /Dist. by Universal Press Syndicate

LALO ALCARAZ

Hey, cuz, it's a trip to be in the action and then watch it on TV.

The Iraqis all watch that "Al-Jazeera" news channel.

What a load of propaganda.

We all watch "Fox News."

4/15 ©2003 LALO ALCARAZ /Dist. by Universal Press Syndicate

LALO ALCARAZ

Chuy, I thought you said this was "Thai food."

Yeah, it's like angel hair "fideo" noodles in Mexican hot sauce.

Did I say "Thai"?

I meant "Thai-Juana."

LALO ALCARAZ 4/16 ©2003 LALO ALCARAZ /Dist. by Universal Press Syndicate

67

Strip 1 (4/17):

YOU KNOW, IF YOU REARRANGED THE FURNITURE A BIT...

I THINK YOU COULD GET MORE SPACE IN YOUR APARTMENT IF YOU JUST ANGLED THE COUCH.

ANGLING THE COUCH WOULD TAKE UP MORE SPACE, VERO.

NO IT WON'T.

LOOK, THIS IS THE ONLY WAY AN ANGLED COUCH WOULD TAKE UP LESS ROOM.

HEY!

LALO ALCARAZ 4/17

©2003 LALO ALCARAZ /Dist. by Universal Press Syndicate

Strip 2 (4/18):

I REALLY THINK YOU COULD USE A LITTLE MORE APPEALING CULTURAL ARTWORK ON THE WALLS.

YOU COULD PUT UP SOME NICE FRIDA POSTERS...

BUT WE'VE ALREADY GOT PLENTY OF FRIDA POSTERS!

SALMA HAYEK BIKINI SHOTS WITH A UNI-BROW DRAWN IN DON'T COUNT!

LALO ALCARAZ 4/18

©2003 LALO ALCARAZ /Dist. by Universal Press Syndicate

Strip 3 (4/19):

LOOK, GUYS. I THOUGHT YOUR APARTMENT NEEDED A LITTLE DECOR, SO I BROUGHT YOU A THROW RUG!

WHY DO THEY CALL THEM "THROW RUGS"?

I'LL SHOW YOU.

LALO ALCARAZ 4/19

©2003 LALO ALCARAZ /Dist. by Universal Press Syndicate

68

Panel 1: I'M TELLING YOU, YOUR FRIEND LUPE IS **CRAZY.** / YOU'RE JUST SAYING THAT BECAUSE SHE'S A WOMAN!

Panel 2: COULD YOU TWO PUT YOUR HANDS DOWN? I CAN'T HEAR MYSELF THINK!

ABIERTO OPEN

4/20

LALO ALCARAZ

Panel 3: HUH? / EVER NOTICE HOW LATINOS TEND TO TALK WITH THEIR HANDS?

Panel 4: NO. / IT'S CALLED **GESTICULATION,** I THINK MANY "LATIN" CULTURES TALK WITH THEIR HANDS.

©2003 LALO ALCARAZ /Dist. by Universal Press Syndicate

Panel 5: WHAT'S YOUR POINT? / I'M JUST SAYING... THERE'S THE RIGHT WAY TO TALK WITH YOUR HANDS, THEN THERE'S **MY** WAY.

Panel 6: ISN'T THAT RIGHT, FELLAS?

69

THE NEW LIST OF THE "100 MOST POWERFUL PEOPLE IN HOLLYWOOD" JUST CAME OUT.

NO.1 IS STEVEN SPIELBERG.

THE LIST OF THE "100 MOST POWERFUL LATINOS IN HOLLYWOOD" JUST CAME OUT, TOO.

WHO'S NO.1?

STEVEN SPIELBERG'S GARDENER.

©2003 LALO ALCARAZ /Dist. by Universal Press Syndicate 4/21

CAN YOU HEAR ME NOW, MIJO?

¡SI, ABUELA!

THAT'S IT. I'M OFFICIALLY THE LAST PERSON IN TOWN WITHOUT A CELL PHONE.

©2003 LALO ALCARAZ /Dist. by Universal Press Syndicate 4/22

AARGH! OUCH! YECH!

WHAT'S WRONG, CUCO?!

I'M TRYING TO SUPPORT FREE SPEECH, BUT IT'S SO PAINFUL.

DIXIE CHICKS.

©2003 LALO ALCARAZ /Dist. by Universal Press Syndicate 4/23

70

Panel 1: SOUTH CENTRAL LOS ANGELES IS GOING TO DROP THE "SOUTH CENTRAL" FROM ITS OFFICIAL NAME.

©2003 LALO ALCARAZ /Dist. by Universal Press Syndicate 4/24

Panel 2: THE CITY COUNCIL THINKS THE NAME CHANGE WILL IMPROVE THE BAD IMAGE OF THE CITY CREATED BY YEARS OF "GANGSTA RAP" IMAGERY.

Panel 3: IN A RELATED MOVE, "INNER-CITY POVERTY" WILL BE CHANGING ITS NAME TO "URBAN CHIC."

Panel 4: BARRIOBUCKS CAFE — BARRIOBUCKS COFFEE AND CHECK CASHING

©2003 LALO ALCARAZ /Dist. by Universal Press Syndicate

Panel 5: I WONDER WHEN THE U.S. WILL FINALLY DO SOMETHING ABOUT URBAN POVERTY?

Panel 6: LALO ALCARAZ 4/25 — WHEN THEY DISCOVER "URBAN OIL."

Panel 7: LALO ALCARAZ 4/26 — IN CASE ANYONE'S INTERESTED, WE'VE GOT A GAME GOING OUT BACK.

©2003 LALO ALCARAZ Dist. by Universal Press Syndicate

71

CLUB ROK·A·MOLE
ESTA NOCHE MOLOTOV·RASCUACHE·BRUJERIA
TIENDITA
LECHE $3

DRESS CODE ?!

ESTE DOMINGO 4/27 CONCIERTO CON TUMBADOS EAST L.A. SABOR FACTORY GO BETTY GO LOS POCHOS EN SMOKIN' MIRRORS HOLLYWOOD Y VERMONT

ESTAF

LALO ALCARAZ 4/27

©2003 LALO ALCARAZ /Dist. by Universal Press Syndicate

72

EFPTO...

ZLPED...

PECF DE...

COULD YOU GET AN EYE CHART THAT'S **NOT** IN SPANISH? THIS ONE'S MAKING **NO** SENSE TO ME.

LALO ALCARAZ 4-28
Dist. by Universal Press Syndicate ©2003 LALO ALCARAZ

SO WHY IS THE PRESIDENT TRYING TO STOP AFFIRMATIVE ACTION?

BECAUSE HE BELIEVES WE ALL HAVE AN "EVEN PLAYING FIELD."

4-29 LALO ALCARAZ

PIONEER ELEMENTARY PLAYGROUND WATCH YOUR STEP

THE PRESIDENT'S NEVER SEEN **OUR** PLAYING FIELD.

©2003 LALO ALCARAZ /Dist. by Universal Press Syndicate

BARRIOBUCKS CAFE
BARRIOBUCKS COFFEE AND CHECK CASHING

©2003 LALO ALCARAZ /Dist. by Universal Press Syndicate

SO THE PRESIDENT WANTS TO GET RID OF AFFIRMATIVE ACTION BECAUSE HE SAYS IT'S **UNFAIR.**

UNFAIR? LIKE PRIVATE TUTORS, EXPENSIVE TEST PREPARATION SERVICES, LEGACY ADMISSIONS, PREFERENTIAL TREATMENT FOR ATHLETES, ETC.?

IT'S FAIR TO SAY THAT.

4-30 LALO ALCARAZ

73

Panel 1: YOU SHOULD JUST SHUT YOUR PEACE HOLE AND SUPPORT THE TROOPS! / SO DAMN INSANE

Panel 2: REALLY? I BET I SUPPORT THE TROOPS MORE THAN YOU DO!!

Panel 3: WHAAT?! / WHY DON'T WE GIVE IMMEDIATE CITIZENSHIP TO EVERY IMMIGRANT SOLDIER? / LALO ALCARAZ 5-1

Panel 4: ©2003 LALO ALCARAZ Dist. by Universal Press Syndicate / UH AH UH AH AH / FINALLY, SOME REAL "SHOCK AND AWE."

Panel 1: WHAT ARE YOU ANYWAY?! / THE U.S. GOVERNMENT MIGHT SAY I'M HISPANIC, OR NOW, LATINO, / IRAQ AND I ROLL / ©2003 LALO ALCARAZ /Dist. by Universal Press Syndicate / LALO ALCARAZ 5-2

Panel 2: TO BE MORE SPECIFIC, I COULD SAY I'M MEXICAN-AMERICAN, THOUGH I PREFER THE MORE POLITICALLY CHARGED TERM CHICANO...

Panel 3: NO, I MEAN, ARE YOU SOME KIND OF GIANT TALKING BUG, OR SHOULD I STOP WITH THE TEQUILA SHOTS?! / DIPSY CHICKS

Panel 1: TITANS / CHUY'S / AZT

Panel 2: WAIT A MINUTE. THIS IS CONFUSING! WHAT DO ALL THESE LABELS MEAN? / LIKE WHAT'S THE DIFFERENCE BETWEEN "HISPANIC" AND "CHICANO"? / ©2003 LALO ALCARAZ /Dist. by Universal Press Syndicate

Panel 3: LALO ALCARAZ 5-3 / ABOUT 50 GRAND A YEAR.

74

Panel 1: CINCO DE MAYO STREET FESTIVAL (YES WE KNOW IT'S MAY 4th TODAY, SO WHAT?)
"DID YOU WIN ANOTHER 'LOWRIDER GUY' MIRROR?"
"YOU CAN'T SAY CINCO DE MAYO DOESN'T BRING ART TO THE PEOPLE."

Panel 2: LALO ALCARAZ 5/4
Sign: CINCO DE MAYO IS UNAMERICAN! DON'T CELEBRATE
"WHAT'S SO UNAMERICAN ABOUT TOO MUCH PARTYING, TOO MUCH SPENDING AND LOTS OF CORPORATE SPONSORSHIPS?"

Panel 3: "WE SHOULDN'T BE CELEBRATING SOME OBSCURE FOREIGN HOLIDAY RIGHT NOW!"
"HEY, PAL, CINCO DE MAYO HAPPENS TO MARK THE MEXICAN DEFEAT IN 1862 OF THE FRENCH."

Panel 4: "CUCO, WHO'S YOUR FRIEND?" "LONG STORY."
Sign: MEXICO #1, FRANCE IS EL STINKO!

©2003 LALO ALCARAZ /Dist. by Universal Press Syndicate

75

©2003 LALO ALCARAZ /Dist. by Universal Press Syndicate

Panel 1: EDDIE, YOU KNOW WHAT DAY IT IS TODAY, RIGHT? / YEAH, MAY 5th.

Panel 2: UH, SORT OF... IT'S THAT SPECIAL DAY WHEN EVERYONE CELEBRATES WITH THEIR FAVORITE YET MOSTLY UNSUNG MINORITY GROUP. / SOME BEERS MAY BE INVOLVED. / OH RIGHT! HOW COULD I FORGET?

LALO ALCARAZ 5/5

Panel 3: HAPPY CARTOONISTS DAY! / HEY! I THOUGHT WE AGREED TO CALL IT "CARTOON DE MAYO"!

www.reuben.org

Panel 4: IN A SIGN THAT LATINO MARKETING HAS SURELY GONE TOO FAR...

5/6 ©2003 LALO ALCARAZ /Dist. by Universal Press Syndicate

Panel 5: THIS NEXT SONG IS BY THE NEWEST BOY BAND...

Panel 6: " 'N SYNCO DE MAYO."

Panel 7: PIONEER ELEMENTARY / TESTING TESTING

LALO ALCARAZ 5/7

©2003 LALO ALCARAZ /Dist. by Universal Press Syndicate

Panel 8: COME ON, CHILDREN. IT'S TESTING TIME!

Panel 9: MRS. RAMOS, DON'T YOU THINK THESE STANDARDIZED TESTS CAN BE A BIT CULTURALLY BIASED AGAINST INNER CITY STUDENTS?

Panel 10: NONSENSE! NOW GET BUSY ADMINISTERING THE EXAM ON THE HISTORY OF AMISH BUGGY MAKING.

76

Strip 1 (5/8):
ANOTHER TEST?! SHOULDN'T WE BE LEARNING MORE STUFF INSTEAD?

NOW JOSÉ, YOU MUST UNDERSTAND, THE HIGHER OUR TEST SCORES, THE HIGHER OUR FUNDING...

AND THE HIGHER THE FUNDING, THE MORE TIME WE CAN SPEND LEARNING...

BETTER TEST-TAKING SKILLS.

Strip 2 (5/9):
BARRIOBUCKS CAFE
BARRIOBUCKS COFFEE AND CHECK CASHING

DID YOU KNOW THEY CHANGED THE TITLE OF THE MOVIE "PAPICHULO" TO "CHASING PAPI" FOR MARKETING REASONS?

WHY? WHAT DOES "PAPICHULO" MEAN?

IT'S SPANISH FOR "STINKEROONIE."

Strip 3 (5/10):
COME ON, YOU GUYS ARE BEING TOO HARD ON "CHASING PAPI."

IT'S A FUN MOVIE WITH A STRONG LATINA CAST.

VERO, IT MAKES "MAID IN MANHATTAN" LOOK LIKE "THE DOLORES HUERTA STORY."

77

MAY 10

FELÍZ DIA DE LAS MADRES, MOM.

OH, ISN'T THAT SWEET... YOU CALL YOUR MOM ON MEXICAN MOTHER'S DAY...

ELAC

MAY 11

I CALL HER BOTH DAYS,

HAPPY, MOTHER'S DAY, MOM.

BECAUSE SHE IS FROM MEXICO, AND IT KEEPS HER HAPPY!

CHICANA

MAY 12

RIIINNGG RIIINNGG RIIIINN

MIJO, WHY DON'T YOU EVER CALL?

©2003 LALO ALCARAZ./Dist. by Universal Press Syndicate
5/11 Feliz Dia de Las Madres CHUY!
LALO ALSARAZ

78

5/12 LALO ALCARAZ

FAILED TO JUMP ON LATINO BANDWAGON

©2003 LALO ALCARAZ /Dist. by Universal Press Syndicate

©2003 LALO ALCARAZ /Dist. by Universal Press Syndicate

LALO ALCARAZ 5/13

US POST OFFICE

GET THE NEW

USA 37

CESAR CHAVEZ STAMP

CHECK THAT STAMP OUT! IT'S ABOUT TIME!!

WHO WOULD HAVE THOUGHT THAT ONE OF THE GREATEST, MOST IMPORTANT MEXICAN-AMERICAN LEADERS OF ALL TIME WOULD BE ON A STAMP?

I GUESS IT **IS** PRETTY COOL.

LET ME HAVE SOME OF THEM NEW LEE TREVINO STAMPS.

©2003 LALO ALCARAZ /Dist. by Universal Press Syndicate

LALO ALCARAZ 5/14

I PREDICT THE CESAR CHAVEZ STAMP WILL BE A BIG SUCCESS!

POST OFFICE

HOW MANY DID **YOU** BUY?

WELL, NONE.

WHO NEEDS STAMPS WHEN YOU'VE GOT E-MAIL?

79

Panel 1: THANKS TO THE EXTREME POST-WAR UNITY SIMPLY RAMPANT IN AMERICA, POLICE OFFICIALS HAVE ANNOUNCED A CHANGE IN CIVIL DISTURBANCE PROCEDURES.

©2003 LALO ALCARAZ /Dist. by Universal Press Syndicate

Panel 2: URBAN RIOTERS TAKE NOTE: WIDESPREAD LOOTING AND RANSACKING WILL NOW BE KNOWN AS...

Panel 3: "THE UNTIDINESS"...

LALO ALCARAZ 5/15

MEANWHILE AT THE **BARRIO BUGLE**...

LALO ALCARAZ 5/16

Panel 1: LOPEZ, DID YOU FINISH THAT LAYOUT OF THE FRONT PAGE?

YES, MR. JEFE, IT TOOK ME **3 HOURS** OF DELICATE LAYOUT WORK TO DO IT.

BARRIO BUGLE — TIENDA

Panel 2: I PUT EVERYTHING ELSE ASIDE TO COMPLETE THE JOB.

Panel 3: WONDERFUL. NOW DUMP IT. WE'RE GOING WITH A NEW STORY ON INEFFICIENCY IN THE WORKPLACE.

©2003 LALO ALCARAZ /Dist. by Universal Press Syndicate

Panel 1: OH, AND DID YOU MAIL OUT THOSE THINGS I ASKED YOU TO?

YES, MR. JEFE. I EVEN USED THE NEW CESAR CHAVEZ STAMPS.

©2003 LALO ALCARAZ /Dist. by Universal Press Syndicate

Panel 2: WHY DON'T WE COVER THE LAUNCH OF THE STAMP?

TOO BORING. WAIT...

Panel 3: I CAN SEE THE HEADLINE: "HISPANIC AGITATOR STAMPED OUT BY FEDS."

LALO ALCARAZ 5/17

80

EDDIE, BUT YOU PROMISED TO GO TO THE MALL WITH ME!

OOOH, QUE MALL-O.

I'M GOING TO CHECK OUT SOME BLOUSES HERE.

I'M GOING TO CHECK OUT HERE.

TRENDYZ

EXCUSE ME, MISS. DO YOU WORK HERE?

SORRY, NO.

LALO ALCARAZ 5/18

©2003 LALO ALCARAZ /Dist. by Universal Press Syndicate

CAN YOU HELP ME, MISS?

NO! I DON'T WORK HERE!

EXCUSE ME...

NO! DO I LOOK LIKE I WORK HERE?!

JUST BECAUSE I AM A YOUNG WOMAN OF COLOR DOESN'T MEAN I WORK AT THIS CLOTHING STORE!

FULL OF REALLY CUTE CLOTHES.

WHAT'S YOUR EMPLOYEE DISCOUNT?

JOB APPLICATIONS

81

WHOA...THERE'S A MAGAZINE FOR EVERYTHING!

MAGAZINES

©2003 LALO ALCARAZ /Dist. by Universal Press Syndicate
5/19
LALO ALCARAZ

ANTIQUE COMPUTERS, PYGMY CINEMA, ASIAN POOL DESIGN, CAT RANCHING...

HERE'S A WHOLE BUNCH OF MAGAZINES DEVOTED TO IGNORING LATINO ISSUES.

TIME, NEWSWEEK, U.S. NEWS...

I CAN'T DECIDE WHAT CAR MAGAZINE I WANT!

STREET CUSTOM, VW CLASSICS, LOWRIDER, BLVD, STREET LOW, IMPORT TUNER...

I NEED A CAR MAGAZINE THAT CUTS OUT ALL THE FILLER AND GETS RIGHT TO THE TOPIC I'M INTERESTED IN!

5/20
LALO ALCARAZ

HERE IT IS... "HOODRATS 'N HOOCHIES."

©2003 LALO ALCARAZ /Dist. by Universal Press Syndicate

SO WHAT ARE YOU GONNA BUY?

BILL BENNETT'S LATEST BOOK.

BOOKS Y LIBROS

BENNET

YOU'RE BUYING "THE BOOK OF VIRTUES"?!

ACTUALLY IT'S CALLED "LAS VEGAS ON $240,000 A DAY."

5/21
LALO ALCARAZ

©2003 LALO ALCARAZ /Dist. by Universal Press Syndicate

82

HEY, TACO CART GUY! HOW'S THE MOBILE RESTAURANT BIZ?

WELL, LIKE WE SAY IN MY LINE OF WORK... WHETHER BUSINESS IS GOOD OR BAD—

©2003 LALO ALCARAZ /Dist. by Universal Press Syndicate

LALO ALCARAZ 5/22

I'M MOVING TACOS.

LALO ALCARAZ 5/23

©2003 LALO ALCARAZ /Dist. by Universal Press Syndicate

I'D LIKE TO EXPAND MY BUSINESS, BUT YOU NEED A BANK LOAN FOR THAT.

THE BANK?! THOSE CROOKS GOUGE POOR PEOPLE IN THE BARRIO WITH SUPER HIGH INTEREST RATES! THEY EVEN MAKE ME SICK!!

WHO WAS THAT?

LOUIE THE LOAN SHARK.

UNEMPLOYMENT IS REALLY UP EVERYWHERE.

©2003 LALO ALCARAZ /Dist. by Universal Press Syndicate

5/24

LALO ALCARAZ

HOW CAN YOU TELL?

MOST IMMIGRANT LABORERS NOW HAVE FOUR LOW-PAYING JOBS INSTEAD OF SIX.

83

IF IT'S CORTEZ, I'M NOT HERE.

LALO ALCARAZ
5/25

©2003 LALO ALCARAZ /Dist. by Universal Press Syndicate

84

Panel 1: DUDE! I JUST SECURED A BILLION-DOLLAR NO-BID CONTRACT TO SUPPLY CHICANO ART FOR THE IRAQI REBUILDING EFFORT!!

WHAT?! HOW DID YOU DO IT?!

I JUST TOLD THEM MY NAME WAS "JOSÉ CHENEY."

5/26

LALO ALCARAZ ©2003 LALO ALCARAZ /Dist. by Universal Press Syndicate

Panel 2: LALO ALCARAZ 5/27 ©2003 LALO ALCARAZ /Dist. by Universal Press Syndicate

MEXICO DESERVES THE "FRENCH TREATMENT" IF YOU ASK ME.

NO ONE ASKED.

EL BUSH DIDN'T HAVE CINCO DE MAYO FESTIVITIES AT THE WHITE HOUSE BECAUSE MEXICO DIDN'T SUPPORT THE IRAQ WAR.

OH NO! AND I HEAR CONGRESS IS RENAMING "TACO BELL" "LIBERTY BELL."

Panel 3: THE PRESIDENT IS ON A ROLL! HE SHOULD GO BEYOND THE WAR ON TERROR.

MAYBE HE COULD START A WAR ON VIOLENCE.

YES! HE SHOULD NUKE VIOLENCE OUT OF EXISTENCE!

5/28

LALO ALCARAZ ©2003 LALO ALCARAZ /Dist. by Universal Press Syndicate

85

UH-OH, THE VIEJITOS ARE AT IT AGAIN...

CHUY'S DINER

★@?!

IT'S TRUE, PEPE, I FOUGHT WITH PANCHO VILLA DURING THE REVOLUTION'S FIERCEST BATTLES!

CHEPE, YOU DIDN'T FIGHT WITH PANCHO VILLA! YOU GOT INTO A SCUFFLE OVER AT PANCHO'S RETIREMENT VILLA!

YES, BUT IT WAS THE FIERCEST INSTANCE OF "WALKER RAGE" YOU'VE EVER SEEN.

5/29
©2003 LALO ALCARAZ /Dist. by Universal Press Syndicate
LALO ALCARAZ

©2003 LALO ALCARAZ /Dist. by Universal Press Syndicate

YUP, I WAS THERE WITH PANCHO VILLA.

DON'T BE-LIEVE THIS OLD FOOL, BOYS!

IN FACT, CUCO, YOU LOOK JUST LIKE PANCHO VILLA'S COUSIN.

NO HE DOESN'T!

HOW WOULD YOU KNOW?

THAT'S WHAT GERONIMO TOLD ME.

5/30
LALO ALCARAZ

HEY, TACO CART GUY. SIX TACOS DE ASADA, PLEASE.

ARE YOU SELLING T-SHIRTS FOR THE FEDERAL TRADE COMMISSION?

FTC
T-SHIRTS $10

CUCO, CUCO, CUCO. I'M AN UNLICENSED STREET VENDOR. WHAT WOULD I BE DOING SELLING SOMETHING LIKE THAT?

NO, THIS IS FOR A HIGHER CAUSE...

FREE TOMMY CHONG
FREE TOMMY CHONG
FTC
TACOS

5/31
LALO ALCARAZ
©2003 LALO ALCARAZ /Dist. by Universal Press Syndicate

86

DO YOU REMEMBER WHAT IT WAS LIKE GROWING UP?

UH-HUH.

WHAT DID WE FILL OUR DAYS WITH?

I'M NOT SURE...

I CAN REMEMBER WATCHING TONS OF TV.

ME TOO. AND LOTS OF HANGING OUT.

THE DAYS SEEMED TO GO SLOWER.

YOU COULD DO MORE IN A DAY.

UH-HUH. BUT I THOUGHT TIME GOES FAST WHEN YOU'RE HAVING FUN?

LALO ALCARAZ 6/1

NOW THE DAYS ZOOM BY... BUT I'M NOT HAVING AS MUCH FUN AS I DID WHEN I WAS A KID.

WE SHOULD SLOW DOWN!

IT MAY BE TOO LATE.

©2003 LALO ALCARAZ /Dist. by Universal Press Syndicate Apologies to Bill Watterson

THAT WAS SURREAL.

MORE LIKE "CALVIN-ESQUE."

87

Panel 1: "AMERICANS SHOULD STRIVE FOR A COLOR-BLIND SOCIETY BY IGNORING A PERSON'S RACE OR ETHNICITY," SAY REPUBLICAN LEADERS. LALO ALCARAZ 6/2

Panel 2: IN A RELATED STORY, REPUBLICAN LEADERS COMMENTED ON THE JOURNALISTIC CRISIS AT THE NEW YORK TIMES, SAYING:

Panel 3: "THAT **BLACK** GUY REALLY MESSED UP, DIDN'T HE? IT'S A **BLACK** DAY FOR JOURNALISM! WHAT A **BLACK** EYE FOR THE NEW YORK TIMES... DID WE MENTION JAYSON BLAIR WAS **BLACK**?"

LALO ALCARAZ 6/3

BARRIO BUGLE
NOW W/ NEWS TICKER
TIENDA

Panel: LOPEZ! DID YOU FINISH CHECKING THAT ARTICLE FOR FACTS?

YES, MR. JEFE.

Panel: I DIDN'T FIND ANY.

Panel: MR. JEFE, AREN'T YOU WORRIED ABOUT JOURNALISTIC INTEGRITY?

THAT ARTICLE I JUST PROOFED WAS FILLED WITH MISSTATEMENTS, DISTORTED FACTS AND INNUENDO.

I KNOW, I KNOW.

BUT IT'S TIME THE BARRIO BUGLE WENT MAINSTREAM!

LALO ALCARAZ 6/4

88

Strip 1 (6/5): ROUGH DAY AT WORK? / OH YEAH, MR. JEFE WANTS THE BARRIO BUGLE TO PRINT MORE SENSATIONALIZED FICTIONAL STORIES. / THAT'S TOO BAD. I THINK NEWSPAPERS SHOULD TRY TO BE MORE LIKE THE NEW YORK TIMES. / OOH LOOK! BAT BOY AND THE CHUPACABRA ARE TEAMING UP TO TACKLE THE MIDDLE EAST SITUATION!

Strip 2 (6/6): TO CUT DOWN ON PIRACY, MAJOR MOVIE STUDIOS ARE ROLLING OUT DVD RENTALS THAT ARE UNWATCHABLE AFTER 48 HOURS. / THAT'S AN IMPROVEMENT. / MOST OF THEIR FILMS ARE UNWATCHABLE THE DAY OF THEIR RELEASE.

Strip 3 (6/7): EXCUSE ME, IS THIS SOME NEW LATINO FASHION LINE? / YES, IT'S OUR DEPARTMENT STORE'S ATTEMPT TO REACH THE LATINA FASHION CONSUMER. / IT'S TIME RETAILERS REACHED OUT. THEY'VE LONG UNDERESTIMATED OUR SIZE. / TELL ME ABOUT IT, GIRL...

89

WHY IS EVERYBODY SITTING AROUND AND MOPING ON SUCH A NICE DAY?

LET'S GO FOR A FUN SUNDAY DRIVE!

TOO CROWDED.

HAVE YOU CLEANED YOUR CAR?

IS IT SAFE?

THERE'S NOTHING LIKE A SUNDAY DRIVE TO CLEAR YOUR MIND OF NEGATIVE THOUGHTS...

COME ON, LET'S GO!

SARDINAS

SEE?! IT'S ONLY BEEN AN HOUR—DON'T YOU FEEL MUCH BETTER?

6/8

LALO ALCARAZ

©2003 LALO ALCARAZ /Dist. by Universal Press Syndicate

90

Panel 1: COLLEGES ARE DROPPING MINORITY STUDENT PROGRAMS DUE TO LEGAL PRESSURE FROM CONSERVATIVES.

SCHOOL

6/9 ©2003 LALO ALCARAZ /Dist. by Universal Press Syndicate

Panel 2: CONSERVATIVES SAY, "DON'T WORRY, KIDS! THERE ARE PLENTY OF PROGRAMS WE'LL NEVER CLOSE, LIKE THE ROTC'S SUMMER GUN FUN CAMP, EVERY INNER-CITY JUVENILE HALL ...

Panel 3: ... AND ANYTHING INCLUDING THE WORDS **AUTO SHOP**."

Panel 4: THE BUSH WHITE HOUSE HAS WARNED EDUCATIONAL INSTITUTIONS **NOT** TO ACTIVELY RECRUIT MINORITY STUDENTS TO INCREASE DIVERSITY.

6/10 ©2003 LALO ALCARAZ /Dist. by Universal Press Syndicate

Panel 5: PRESIDENT BUSH SAID, "THERE'S PLENTY OF INSTITUTIONS OF HIGHER LEARNING THAT HAVE ACHIEVED DIVERSITY WITHOUT AFFIRMATIVE ACTION."

Panel 6: HE MADE THESE REMARKS AS COMMENCEMENT SPEAKER AT **McDONALD'S UNIVERSITY.**

Panel 7: UH, TACO CART GUY, DO YOU HAVE ANYTHING BESIDES BEEF?

DON'T TELL ME YOU ARE THINKING ABOUT THE **MAD COW?**

Panel 8: HAVE NO FEAR. I USE ONLY THE FINEST AMERICAN BEEF FOR MY TACOS, NEVER THAT CHEAP CANADIAN STUFF.

GOOD! BECAUSE WE WERE WORRIED ABOUT OUR HEALTH.

6/11

TACOS

Panel 9: EIGHT TACOS, PLEASE, EXTRA LARD.

CAN YOU WRAP MY TACOS IN BACON?

91

6/12

Panel 1: I UNDERSTAND YOU BOYS ARE CONCERNED ABOUT **MAD COW...**

WITH ALL THAT SENSATIONAL NEWS COVERAGE.

TACOS

©2003 LALO ALCARAZ /Dist. by Universal Press Syndicate

LALO ALCARAZ

Panel 2: I, TOO, WAS CONSTANTLY IN FEAR OF THE MAD COW...

UNTIL I DIVORCED HER.

TACOS

6/13

LALO ALCARAZ

MALL

JUDGE JUDY LOVES OUR FOOD COURT

GIRL, YOU'RE ALWAYS IN THIS CLOTHING STORE OR WINDOW SHOPPING IN THE MALL...

I BLAME THE MAN THAT DRAWS ME.

YOU MEAN THE CARTOONIST?

NO. CALVIN KLEIN.

©2003 LALO ALCARAZ /Dist. by Universal Press Syndicate

©2003 LALO ALCARAZ /Dist. by Universal Press Syndicate

LALO ALCARAZ **6/14**

WHERE'S THE SWIMWEAR SECTION?

JUST LISTEN FOR IT...

AAAAARGH!

WHAT WAS **THAT?!**

IT'S JUST THIS CRAZY GRINGA. EVERY SUMMER IT'S THE SAME THING...

BE RIGHT THERE, MA'AM.

92

AUTO PARTS FEEL FREE TO WORK ON YOUR DIRTY CAR IN THE PARKING LOT

I GOTTA STOP HERE, VERO.

OKAY.

WHAT ARE YOU BUYING, EDDIE?

MY DAD'S FATHER'S DAY GIFT.

YOU DON'T GET HIM AN ELECTRONIC GADGET OR A TIE?

HE DOESN'T "GET" GADGETS, AND YOU CAN'T USE TIES WITH MEXICAN LEISURE PANT SUITS.

THANKS FOR THE ARMORALL, MIJO! IT WILL KEEP MY SUIT GLOSSY AND WEATHERPROOF!

FELIZ DIA DE LOS PADRES TO ALL!

LALO ALCARAZ 6/15

93

DOLORES, I'M SO GLAD WE COULD MEET FOR COFFEE.

ME TOO. YOU'D THINK COUSINS WOULD STAY IN TOUCH.

THIS NEIGHBORHOOD IS SO "LATIN." I WAS A LITTLE SCARED COMING HERE.

DOLORES SANCHEZ! YOU GREW UP AROUND THE CORNER FROM HERE!

VERONICA, PLEASE CALL ME "DOLLY ST. JAMES." THAT'S MY STAGE NAME.

WELL, YOU'LL NEED IT BECAUSE YOU'RE GOING THROUGH A REALLY WEIRD STAGE.

6-16

DOLORES, WHAT'S UP WITH THIS "DOLLY ST. JAMES" STAGE NAME?

I WANT HOLLYWOOD TO KNOW THAT I'M AN ACTOR, NOT A LATINO ACTOR.

A HA... LOOK, THERE'S A BIG TV CASTING CALL FOR "LATINA TYPES" TODAY...

"DOLLY."

6-17

PLEASE USE MY FULL NAME: DOLORES ROSARIO MARIA CONCHITA ALONSO GONZALEZ SANCHEZ!

6-18

IF I TRY OUT FOR ALL THESE LATINA ROLES, I'LL HAVE TO DYE MY HAIR BACK TO BLACK...

LOSE THE BLUE CONTACTS...

AND STOP HIDING FROM THE SUN.

IT'S HARD BEING LATINA! HOW DO YOU DO IT?

I WAKE UP AND PUT ON MY SOMBRERO ONE LEG AT A TIME, JUST LIKE EVERYBODY ELSE.

94

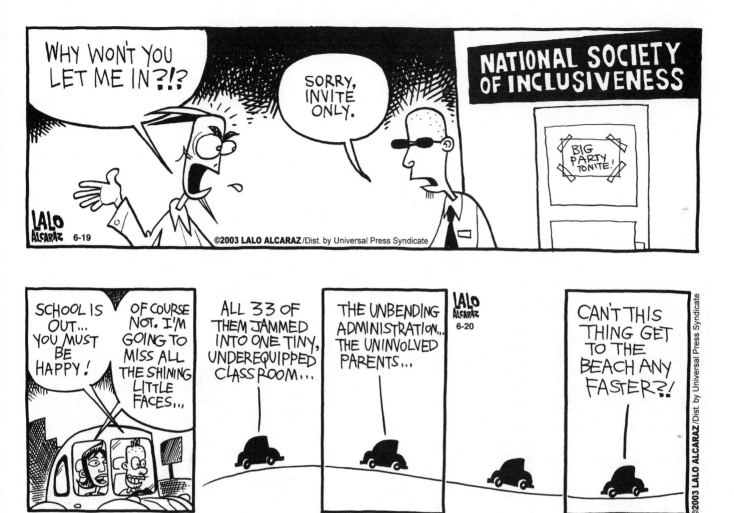

Panel 1: WHY WON'T YOU LET ME IN ?!? — SORRY, INVITE ONLY.

LALO ALCARAZ 6-19

©2003 LALO ALCARAZ/Dist. by Universal Press Syndicate

Panel 2: NATIONAL SOCIETY OF INCLUSIVENESS — BIG PARTY TONITE!

Panel 3: SCHOOL IS OUT... YOU MUST BE HAPPY! — OF COURSE NOT. I'M GOING TO MISS ALL THE SHINING LITTLE FACES...

Panel 4: ALL 33 OF THEM JAMMED INTO ONE TINY, UNDEREQUIPPED CLASSROOM...

Panel 5: THE UNBENDING ADMINISTRATION... THE UNINVOLVED PARENTS...

LALO ALCARAZ 6-20

Panel 6: CAN'T THIS THING GET TO THE BEACH ANY FASTER?!

©2003 LALO ALCARAZ/Dist. by Universal Press Syndicate

Panel 7: WHAT ARE YOU WATCHING? — UNIVISION.

Panel 8: I THOUGHT YOU HATED SPANISH-LANGUAGE TV! — I DO. BUT NOW, THANKS TO THE F.C.C...

©2003 LALO ALCARAZ/Dist. by Universal Press Syndicate

Panel 9: EVERYTHING IS CALLED "UNIVISION."

LALO ALCARAZ 6-21

95

©2003 LALO ALCARAZ / Dist. by Universal Press Syndicate
LALO ALCARAZ
6/22

Panel 1: MALL — WHERE EVEN MOM AND POP SHOP 'TIL THEY DROP

Panel 2: SO THIS CLOTHING LINE IS AIMED AT LATINAS? — YES, IT'S THE LATEST THING. ALL THE RETAIL CHAINS ARE DOING IT. — CHICA LOCA

Panel 3: LATINOS SPEND AROUND $600 BILLION A YEAR — AND IT'S GROWING. — HAVE YOU SEEN MY CREDIT CARD BILL? IT'S MORE.

Panel 4: BUT I DON'T KNOW ABOUT SOME OF THESE CLOTHES. THEY'RE KIND OF LOUD AND "RUFFLE-ISH". — THEY REFLECT THE LATINO INFLUENCE ON MAINSTREAM FASHION. SO SEXY!

Panel 5: TRY SOME ON! AND DON'T FORGET ALL THE COLORFUL NEW LATINO-THEMED ACCESSORIES!

Panel 6: HOW DO YOU LIKE IT? — I FEEL LIKE A LATINA CELEBRITY. — REALLY? LIKE WHO? J.LO? THALIA? SHAKIRA?

Panel 7: NO, CHIQUITA BANANA.

96

Strip 1 (6/23):

THE **I.N.S.** IS NO LONGER. IT'S BEEN SWALLOWED UP BY THE NEW DEPARTMENT OF HOMELAND SECURITY.

IS THAT BAD?

I DON'T KNOW. WHY DON'T WE ASK THAT INS AGENT OVER THERE?

MY NAME IS AGENT SMITH. I AM NEW TO THIS MATRIX, er, BARRIO.

©2003 LALO ALCARAZ /Dist. by Universal Press Syndicate

Strip 2 (6/24):

NO, CITIZEN, THE I.N.S. MISSION WILL NOT BE AFFECTED BY THE "WAR ON TERROR."

WE ARE EVEN IMPROVING OUR ALREADY EFFICIENT APPROACH TO HELPING OUT IMMIGRANTS.

YOU WILL TAKE US TO YOUR TERROR CELL NOW.

©2003 LALO ALCARAZ /Dist. by Universal Press Syndicate

Strip 3 (6/25):

SO NOW THAT SUSPECTED BOMBER ERIC RUDOLPH HAS BEEN CAPTURED, WILL YOU BE PROFILING YOUNG WHITE MALES AS TERRORIST SUSPECTS?

ERIC **WHO**-DOLPH?

©2003 LALO ALCARAZ /Dist. by Universal Press Syndicate

97

OUCH! THIS IS HOT!

WIMP! YOU THINK THAT'S HOT? I CAN EAT THREE!

OUCH! OUCH, OUCH! THAT'S HOT!

HA! YOU'RE NOT SO TOUGH! I CAN TRY SIX AT A TIME!

OW! MOUTH ON FIRE!

HOT! OUCH! HOT HOT!

THIS CONFIRMS MY THEORY THAT JALAPEÑOS ARE NOT "BRAIN FOOD."

©2003 LALO ALCARAZ /Dist. by Universal Press Syndicate
6/26

TACOS

YOU OKAY, EDDIE?

NO MORE JALAPEÑOS...

©2003 LALO ALCARAZ /Dist. by Universal Press Syndicate
6/27

SO, TITAN, DO YOU STILL PLAY THE PONIES?

NO...

I STICK WITH MY DOGS.

©2003 LALO ALCARAZ /Dist. by Universal Press Syndicate
6/28

98

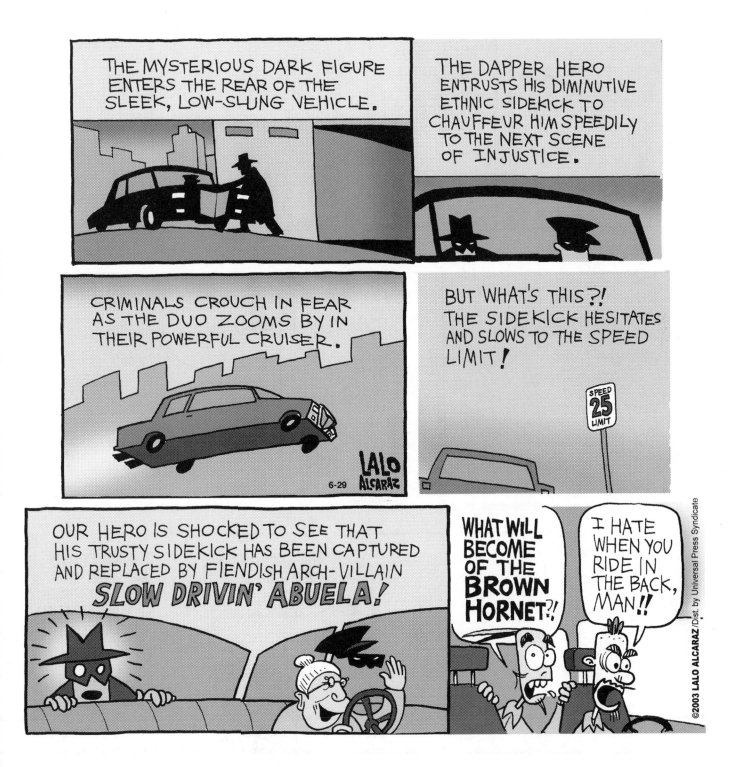

THE MYSTERIOUS DARK FIGURE ENTERS THE REAR OF THE SLEEK, LOW-SLUNG VEHICLE.

THE DAPPER HERO ENTRUSTS HIS DIMINUTIVE ETHNIC SIDEKICK TO CHAUFFEUR HIM SPEEDILY TO THE NEXT SCENE OF INJUSTICE.

CRIMINALS CROUCH IN FEAR AS THE DUO ZOOMS BY IN THEIR POWERFUL CRUISER.

BUT WHAT'S THIS?! THE SIDEKICK HESITATES AND SLOWS TO THE SPEED LIMIT!

SPEED 25 LIMIT

LALO ALCARAZ
6-29

OUR HERO IS SHOCKED TO SEE THAT HIS TRUSTY SIDEKICK HAS BEEN CAPTURED AND REPLACED BY FIENDISH ARCH-VILLAIN *SLOW DRIVIN' ABUELA!*

WHAT WILL BECOME OF THE BROWN HORNET?!

I HATE WHEN YOU RIDE IN THE BACK, MAN!!

©2003 LALO ALCARAZ /Dist. by Universal Press Syndicate

99

WHY DO SO MANY COMIC STRIPS HAVE, LIKE, **ONE** BLACK CHARACTER?

THAT'S TRUE, MIKE. THEY ADD A LAME CHARACTER TO "DIVERSIFY" THEIR STRIPS.

IT'S WEAK TOKENISM BY NON-BLACK CARTOONISTS!

WHAT'S EVERYBODY LOOKING AT?

AND THESE TOKEN BLACK COMIC STRIP CHARACTERS ALL SPEAK IN A FLAT, SANITIZED MANNER!

WORD.

THEY NEVER SPEAK IN ANY KIND OF URBAN SLANG OR HAVE ANY TRACE OF "FLAVOR"!

"FLAVA".

IT IS SIMPLY PREPOSTEROUS!

FOR SHIZZLE MY SHNIZZLE!

TRUE DAT!

BARRIOBUCKS CAFE

BARRIOBUCKS COFFEE AND CHECK CASHING

THIS IS EITHER THE WORLD'S SLOWEST COFFEE LINE...

OR **DAY OF THE DEAD** IS NOW IN JULY.

THERE COULD ALSO BE A SUPERMODEL CONVENTION IN TOWN.

100

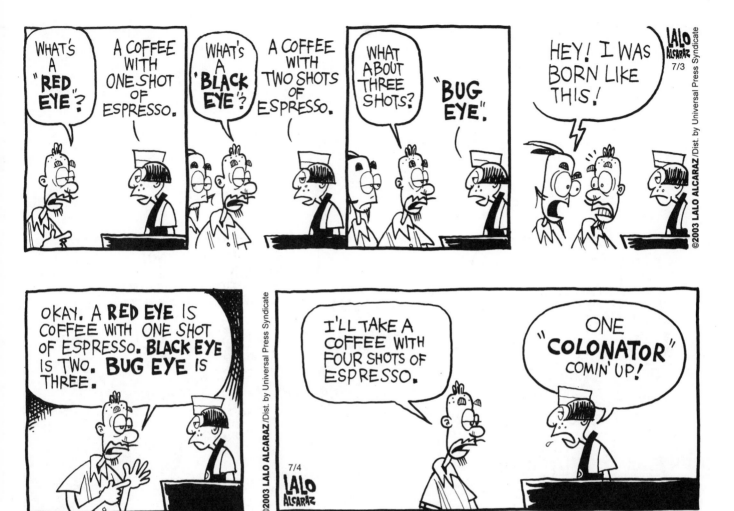

Panel 1: WHAT'S A "RED EYE"? / A COFFEE WITH ONE SHOT OF ESPRESSO.

Panel 2: WHAT'S A "BLACK EYE"? / A COFFEE WITH TWO SHOTS OF ESPRESSO.

Panel 3: WHAT ABOUT THREE SHOTS? / "BUG EYE".

Panel 4: HEY! I WAS BORN LIKE THIS!

7/3

©2003 LALO ALCARAZ/Dist. by Universal Press Syndicate

Panel 5: OKAY. A RED EYE IS COFFEE WITH ONE SHOT OF ESPRESSO. BLACK EYE IS TWO. BUG EYE IS THREE.

©2003 LALO ALCARAZ/Dist. by Universal Press Syndicate

7/4

Panel 6: I'LL TAKE A COFFEE WITH FOUR SHOTS OF ESPRESSO. / ONE "COLONATOR" COMIN' UP!

CLUB / LIVE TONITE / HONG KONG'S THE SARS / FROM ENGLAND: MAD COW / WITH MONKEYPOX

COOL! THAT'S GONNA BE A SICK SHOW!

©2003 LALO ALCARAZ/ Dist. by Universal Press Syndicate

7/5

101

"...AND A SMALL GROUP OF FREEDOM FIGHTERS OVER-THREW THE SHACKLES OF OPPRESSION IMPOSED BY THEIR IMPERIALIST OVERLORDS...

CUCO! CAN YOU NOT DISCUSS POLITICS, REVOLUTION OR IMPERIALISM FOR JUST ONE DAY?!

IT IS THE FOURTH OF JULY AFTER ALL...

KISS THE COCINERO

7/6

LALO ALCARAZ ©2003 LALO ALCARAZ/Dist. by Universal Press Syndicate

102

Panel 1: DEAR COUSIN EDDIE,

Panel 2: IT'S YOUR PRIMO CHAVA. I'M STILL OUT HERE IN IRAQ. I AM OKAY.

Panel 3: WE'RE STILL LOOKING FOR WEAPONS OF MASS DESTRUCTION, THOUGH NOT AS MUCH RECENTLY. 7-7

Panel 4: IN FACT, SOME OF US HAVE BEEN CATCHING UP ON OUR LETTER-WRITING.

©2003 LALO ALCARAZ /Dist. by Universal Press Syndicate

Panel 5: I'VE BEEN FOLLOWING THE NEWS, PRIMO. LALO ALCARAZ 7-8

Panel 6: I'M SURE YOU'VE HEARD THAT LATINOS ARE NOW THE BIGGEST MINORITY...

Panel 7: BUT ENOUGH ABOUT OUR FRONT LINES.

©2003 LALO ALCARAZ /Dist. by Universal Press Syndicate

Panel 8: A NEWPORT BEACH, CALIFORNIA, CITY COUNCILMAN OPPOSES ADDING GRASS AREAS TO A LOCAL STATE BEACH.

©2003 LALO ALCARAZ /Dist. by Universal Press Syndicate LALO ALCARAZ 7-9

Panel 9: HE SAID THAT "WITH GRASS, WE USUALLY GET MEXICANS COMING IN THERE EARLY IN THE MORNING, AND THEY CLAIM IT AS THEIRS, AND IT BECOMES THEIR PERSONAL, PRIVATE GROUNDS ALL DAY."

Panel 10: HE MAY PASS A COMPROMISE BILL ALLOWING "MEXICANS" ON THE GRASS **ONLY** IF THEY ARE ACCOMPANIED BY A MOWER OR A LEAF BLOWER.

LALO ALSARAZ 7/13

©2003 **LALO ALCARAZ**/Dist. by Universal Press Syndicate

TITANS AZ

CUCO, WHO'S YOUR FRIEND?

SOME GREEN-GO.

105

I TOOK MY OWN CENSUS OF TV...

I FOUND THAT THE LARGEST ETHNIC GROUP ON TV SEEMS TO BE...

SEXY 25-YEAR-OLDS.

AND ALTHOUGH LATINOS ARE **13%** OF THE POPULATION...

IF AMERICA WAS MORE LIKE TV...

ALL LATINOS WOULD LIVE AT **GEORGE LOPEZ'S** HOUSE,

NOW, HOW CAN YOU REALLY SAY THAT LATINOS ARE THE LARGEST **MINORITY** GROUP...

IF LOTS OF LATINOS IDENTIFY THEMSELVES AS "WHITE"?

WELL, MIKE, LATINOS ARE THE **LARGEST** MINORITY...

NOT THE **SMARTEST.**

THANKS, HUEY!

106

Strip 1 (7-17):

AND WHAT ABOUT THE **AFRO-LATINOS?!** IF YOU HAVEN'T NOTICED, THEY'RE BLACK TOO!

DO THEY COUNT DOUBLE?

OR DO THEY AUTOMATICALLY GO TO THE LATINO PILE?

THEY'RE JUST CENSUS NUMBERS, MIKE... KICK BACK.

WHO DID THIS COUNT ANYWAY, **KATHERINE HARRIS?**

Strip 2 (7-18):

SOME MOVIE SEQUEL TITLES JUST SCREAM OUT: **DON'T WATCH ME!**

WHAT, LIKE, "**TERMINATOR 3: I'M RUNNING FOR GOVERNOR**"?

OR "**FRIDAY 6:** FRIDAY AFTER NEXT AFTER NEXT"?

OR "**ALIEN** VS. **PREDATOR:** THE JOHN ASHCROFT STORY"?

OR "**DIRTY DANCING:** HAVANA NIGHTS"?

HEY COME ON, DON'T JOKE AROUND LIKE THAT.

Strip 3 (7-19):

♪ LA CUCARACHA LA CUCARACHA ♫

I LIKE THIS RADIO SHOW, BUT WHEN THEY HAVE A LATINO ON IT, THEY ALWAYS PLAY "LA CUCARACHA" IN THE BACKGROUND.

YEAH, I NOTICED.

I'M SURPRISED YOU HAVEN'T SCREAMED "BIGOTRY."

NAW. TO ME IT'S JUST "BRANDING."

107

DO WE HAVE EVERYTHING WE NEED FOR OUR CARNE ASADA COOKOUT?

CARNE ASADA, CARNE ASADA AND CARNE ASADA.

MEAT

HEY! YOU KNOW WHAT WE NEED IS AN AFTER-MEAL TREAT...

PLAYING CARDS!

7/20

LALO ALCARAZ ©2003 LALO ALCARAZ/Dist. by Universal Press Syndicate

SEMI CONVENIENCE STORE

WHERE'S YOUR PLAYING CARDS?

OUR SCHOOLS WIN LOTERIA WHILE YOU LOSE!

PLAYING CARDS

"IRAQ'S MOST WANTED PLAYING CARDS, THE DECK OF HOLLYWOOD WEASELS, DECK O' CORPORATE SCUMBAGS, STOP LA HILLARY CLINTON CARDS..."

DON'T YOU HAVE ANY NORMAL CARDS WITH, LIKE, KINGS, QUEENS AND JOKERS?!

HERE.

"PRINCE WILLIAM'S ROYAL GIRLFRIENDS PLAYING CARDS."

108

LALO ALCARAZ 7/21

MALL
DID WE MENTION 'UNMENTIONABLES'?

I THINK THESE VICTORIA'S SECRETS DISPLAYS ARE GETTING A BIT RACY... DON'T YOU AGREE, GUYS?

GUYS?

LE OVERPRICED

PANTALON

©2003 LALO ALCARAZ/Dist. by Universal Press Syndicate

THERE SHOULD BE LATINO-OWNED AND OPERATED LINGERIE STORES!

SURE, CUCO.

YOU'LL HAVE TO SETTLE FOR LATINO CELEBRITY ENDORSED LINGERIE...

THE SAMMY SOSA WONDER BRA

YOU'LL SWEAR IT'S NOT FILLED WITH CORK!

LALO ALCARAZ 7/22
©2003 LALO ALCARAZ /Dist. by Universal Press Syndicate

THEATER

I'M SORRY, SIR. WE DON'T ALLOW OUTSIDE FOOD.

WHAT? I'M NOT BRINGING IN ANY OUTSIDE FOOD!

WHO IS HE?

OH, YOU MEAN MY CHILD, AGE 0-2?

LALO ALCARAZ 7/23

TACOS

©2003 LALO ALCARAZ/Dist. by Universal Press Syndicate

109

Panel 1: ARE THESE MOVIE PREVIEWS **EVER** GONNA END?!

7/24

Panel 2: AND NOW IT'S TIME FOR OUR FEATURE PRESENTATION...

Panel 3: A SERIES OF COMMERCIALS JUST LIKE THE ONES ON TV!

©2003 LALO ALCARAZ/Dist. by Universal Press Syndicate

Panel 4: HOW MANY PREVIEWS DO WE HAVE TO WATCH? FROM THE MAKERS OF "**LEGALLY BLONDE II**"...

Panel 5: AND THE PEOPLE WHO BROUGHT YOU "**PATRIOT ACT II**" ... IT'S

Panel 6: "**ILLEGALLY BROWN III**: FULL THROTTLE ROUNDUP"!

7/25

©2003 **LALO ALCARAZ**/Dist. by Universal Press Syndicate

Panel 7: AND ALSO COMING SOON, FROM THE MAKERS OF "**DUMB** AND **DUMBERER**"...

7/26

©2003 LALO ALCARAZ/Dist. by Universal Press Syndicate

Panel 8: AND THE PRODUCERS OF THE **BUSH TAX CUT**...

Panel 9: IT'S "**DUDE, WHERE'S MY JOB?**"

110

LATINOS ARE OFFICIALLY THE NATION'S BIGGEST MINORITY GROUP!

WHO ARE THEY KIDDING? AS IF THAT'S SOME BIG HONOR!

RING RING RIIIII

©2003 LALO ALCARAZ/Dist. by Universal Press Syndicate

7-27

LALO ALCARAZ

CONGRATULATIONS ON BEING THE LARGEST MINORITY GROUP!

WE WOULD LIKE TO PRESENT YOU WITH THIS OVER-SIZED, NON-NEGOTIABLE PHONY CHECK!

PRIZE PATROL
PAY TO THE ORDER OF LATINOS
A MILLION TRILLION DOLLARS

SLAM

SEE, I TOLD YOU IT PAYS TO BUY THE MAGAZINE SUBSCRIPTIONS.

¿?

111

Comic strip (7/28): © 2003 LALO ALCARAZ / Dist. by Universal Press Syndicate

Panel 1: THE AVERAGE TEACHER MAKES $45,000 A YEAR AND IS A WHITE, 42-YEAR-OLD FEMALE.

Panel 2: WOW... WHAT WOULD HAPPEN IF TEACHERS MADE $100,000 A YEAR?

Panel 3: THE WORLD'S BIGGEST SEX CHANGE.

Comic strip (7/29): © 2003 LALO ALCARAZ / Dist. by Universal Press Syndicate

Panel 1: PRESIDENT BUSH IS ASSURING AMERICANS THAT HE HAS FOUND "DARN GOOD" EVIDENCE LINKING IRAQ AND AL-QAIDA.

Panel 2: THE PRESIDENT SAYS, "JUST CHECK OUT THE LYRICS TO COUNTRY SINGER DARRYL WORLEY'S SONG, 'HAVE YOU FORGOTTEN?'"

Panel 3: "IT'S 'DARN GOOD' EVIDENCE, MAYBE EVEN 'DANG GOOD.'"

Comic strip (7/30): © 2003 LALO ALCARAZ / Dist. by Universal Press Syndicate

Panel 1: MEET MY COUSIN MEMO. ¡HOLA! YOU LOOK VERY FUNNY, MY FRIEND!

Panel 3: AND YOU ARE SUCH A STYLISH DRESSER. WHAT IS YOUR SECRET? POLYESTER BEAN BERRY BERRY GOOD TO ME!

112

¡COMPADRE! ¡VAMONOS! DRINKS FIRST, THEN WE GO TO THE **CUCHI CUCHI CLUB** FOR "GORLS"!

WHAT'S UP WITH YOUR COUSIN MEMO, EDDIE?

UH, HE'S A LITTLE TOO OUTGOING.

¡ANDALE! I WANT TO GO TO THE NIGHTCLUB! CAN SOMEBODY TAKE A MEMO?!

7/31

©2003 LALO ALCARAZ /Dist. by Universal Press Syndicate

HEY, THERE GOES A REALLY DOPE PORSCHE!

YEAH, SO?

DIDN'T YOU USE TO FIEND FOR THOSE?

NAW. I GREW OUT OF THAT. IT'S PATHETIC TO LUST FOR MATERIAL STUFF LIKE SPORTS CARS.

NOW I'D RATHER GET A BIG **S.U.V.** WITH SPINNING TWENTY-INCH RIMS.

8/1

©2003 LALO ALCARAZ /Dist. by Universal Press Syndicate

EDDIE, EDDIE, EDDIE. CAN'T YOU HAVE A LESS WASTEFUL FANTASY CAR THAN A BIG S.U.V.?

S.U.V.s ARE GAS HOGS. IT'S JUST NOT AN ECOLOGICALLY FRIENDLY FANTASY.

HAVE YOU CONSIDERED A HYBRID CAR? HOW ABOUT—

OKAY, OKAY! I'VE GOT A NEW, LESS POLLUTING FANTASY!

8/2

©2003 LALO ALCARAZ / Dist. by Universal Press Syndicate

113

SHOW-OFF.

WILL YOU **PLEASE** STOP ROLLING BACK AND FORTH OVER THAT SPEED BUMP?!

I GOTTA GET HYDRAULICS ON THIS THING...

LALO ALCARAZ 8/3

114

Strip 1 (8/4):

Panel 1: (Sign: BARRIOBUCKS CAFE — BARRIOBUCKS COFFEE AND CHECK CASHING) — LALO ALCARAZ 8/4 — ©2003 /Dist. by Universal Press Syndicate

EDDIE, I CAN'T BELIEVE CELIA CRUZ IS GONE.

Panel 2: SOMEHOW I FEEL LIKE SHE'S STILL WITH US... WANT ANYTHING IN YOUR COFFEE?

Panel 3: ¡AZÚCAR!

Strip 2 (8/5):

Panel 1: THAT'S IT! I'M CREATING A REALITY TV SHOW TO PITCH TO THESE DESPERATE NETWORKS!

Panel 2: IT'LL BE THE FIRST TO FEATURE SMART, VIVACIOUS GO-GETTER LATINOS!

Panel 3: (no dialogue)

Panel 4: I'D BETTER GO FIND SOME... HEY! DON'T ALIENATE YOUR POTENTIAL AUDIENCE! — LALO ALCARAZ 8/5 — ©2003 LALO ALCARAZ /Dist. by Universal Press Syndicate

Strip 3 (8/6):

Panel 1: DEAR MR. ROCHA, REGARDING YOUR REALITY TV SHOW IDEA...

Panel 2: THE LATINO SUBJECTS IN YOUR VIDEO ARE NOT IN GANGS, AREN'T ILLEGAL IMMIGRANTS AND THEY DON'T HAVE HEAVY ACCENTS. — 8/6 — ©2003 LALO ALCARAZ /Dist. by Universal Press Syndicate

Panel 3: PERHAPS YOU HAVE US CONFUSED WITH THE SCI-FI CHANNEL.

115

WHAT'S WRONG WITH EDDIE?

HE JUST FOUND OUT THAT THE VW BEETLE HAS BEEN PHASED OUT OF PRODUCTION.

LALO ALCARAZ 8/7

©2003 LALO ALCARAZ /Dist. by Universal Press Syndicate

THEY STOPPED MAKING VW BUGS... WHAT IF THEY STOP MAKING VW PARTS?

HOW AM I GOING TO KEEP MY CAR RUNNING?

LALO ALCARAZ 8/8

DON'T WORRY, EDDIE... THEY STOPPED MAKING VWs, NOT RUBBER BANDS.

©2003 LALO ALCARAZ /Dist. by Universal Press Syndicate

DEMOCRATS ARE ACCUSING REPUBLICANS OF IGNORING THE LATINO VOTER...

"REPUBLICANS ARE ONLY CAPABLE OF SUPERFICIAL, EMPTY GESTURES WHEN COURTING THE LATINO VOTE..."

LALO ALCARAZ 8/9

SAID "RICARDO" GEPHARDT, "JUAN" KERRY AND HOWARD "REFRIED" DEAN.

©2003 LALO ALCARAZ /Dist. by Universal Press Syndicate

116

HO HUM

MAN, JOSÉ, SUMMER IS SOOOOOO BORING...

I GUESS SO, CHATO.

THERE'S NOTHING TO DO OUTSIDE... I WISH I COULD GO HOME AND LIE ON THE COUCH.

©2003 LALO ALCARAZ/Dist. by Universal Press Syndicate

I WISH SCHOOL WAS IN.

WHAT?!

YOU'RE CRAZY, DUDE! WHAT ARE YOU TALKING ABOUT?!

I LIKE SCHOOL, OKAY?

I MISS MY TEACHER.

YOU'RE IN LOVE WITH YOUR TEACHER!

I AM NOT!

CHILL OUT, HOMIE...

MY PARENTS WON'T EVEN LET ME SEE MY TEACHER ANYMORE...

SO I MISS MY TEACHER TOO.

8/10

LALO ALCARAZ

117

THE MAKERS OF IPECAC SYRUP ARE ACCUSING HOLLYWOOD OF UNFAIR COMPETITION.

THEY CLAIM HOLLYWOOD'S LATEST PRODUCT ALSO UPSETS STOMACHS TO THE POINT OF NAUSEA...

"GIGLI."

SUMMER IS GREAT, EXCEPT...

THERE'S NOTHING TO DO...

AND NOWHERE TO GO.

WHY DON'T WE SELL SOMETHING, JOSE?

YEAH! HOW ABOUT LEMONADE?

THAT'S WAY OLD SCHOOL. I WAS THINKIN' BOOTLEG SODAS...

CHATO! THAT'S NOT RIGHT!

YOU'RE RIGHT. I MEANT TO SAY BOOTLEG DVDs.

©2003 LALO ALCARAZ /Dist. by Universal Press Syndicate

8/11
8/12
8/13

LALO ALCARAZ

TACO CART GUY! WHERE HAVE YOU BEEN?!

VACATION.

ACTUALLY, I TRAVELED THE GLOBE SAMPLING THE WORLD'S CUISINE TO SEE HOW I COULD IMPROVE MY MENU.

TACOS

WHAT DID YOU LEARN?

"HAGGIS" IS SCOTTISH MENUDO.

TACOS

8/14

©2003 LALO ALCARAZ /Dist. by Universal Press Syndicate

I WAS ALSO IN PARIS DURING MY SUMMER VACATION...

THAT'S A PHOTO OF WHEN THE EIFFEL TOWER CAUGHT ON FIRE!

I BURNT THE BEARNAISE SAUCE.

©2003 LALO ALCARAZ /Dist. by Universal Press Syndicate 8/15

I VISITED TOKYO, TOO.

8/16

I ORDERED A TACO, AND THE CHEF GAVE ME OCTOPUS.

<HERE IS YOUR TAKO.>

SO I ORDERED FISH AND HE FORGOT TO COOK IT.

<HERE IS YOUR SUSHI.>

YOU DIDN'T FRY IT UP IN FRONT OF HIM, DID YOU?

I HAD TO DEFEND MYSELF USING "TACO KWON DO."

©2003 LALO ALCARAZ /Dist. by Universal Press Syndicate

119

©2003 LALO ALCARAZ /Dist. by Universal Press Syndicate

LALO ALCARAZ 8/18

AN ANTIQUE BELT BUCKLE WOULD SURE SPRUCE UP OLD JEANS!

I JUST LOVE THIS SHOW!

YOU MEAN, UH, UHM, THE, ER, MAKEOVER SHOW FOR STRAIGHT GUYS BY, EH, FAIRLY FLAMBOYANT FELLAS?

GEE, CUCO, THAT'S A REAL NON-CONTROVERSIAL COMICS PAGE WAY OF PUTTING IT.

LALO ALCARAZ 8/19
©2003 LALO ALCARAZ /Dist. by Universal Press Syndicate

I THINK THAT MAKEOVER TV SHOW IS A GREAT IDEA...

IN FACT, IT'S SO GOOD I'M GONNA BITE IT!

"BROWN EYE FOR THE WHITE GUY"!

THAT TITLE NEEDS A DO-OVER.

"MAKEOVER."

©2003 LALO ALCARAZ /Dist. by Universal Press Syndicate

AND WE'RE BACK TO "LATIN EYE FOR THE GRINGO GUY"...

THE MAKEOVER SHOW FOR PEOPLE WHO WANT TO LIVE THE STYLISH LATINO LIFESTYLE...

WHAT?! EACH WEEK YOU'LL SUGGEST A DIFFERENT COLORED GUAYABERA SHIRT?

HEY! GET OUT OF MY IMAGINARY TV SCREEN!

LALO ALCARAZ 8/20

121

Panel 1: WELCOME BACK TO "**LATIN EYE FOR THE GRINGO GUY**"! ©2003 LALO ALCARAZ 8/21

Panel 2: OUR FIRST SUBJECT IS "**RED**", A LOCAL GUY BADLY IN NEED OF A "LATINO MAKEOVER"!

Panel 3: I GOT NOTHING AGAINST YOUR "LATINO LIFESTYLE." I JUST DON'T GET WHY YOU HAVE TO FLAUNT IT IN MY FACE CONSTANTLY! / LIKE IT'S NORMAL...

Panel 4: LT. GOVERNOR CRUZ BUSTAMANTE CAN BE THE FIRST LATINO GOVERNOR OF CALIFORNIA IN MODERN TIMES! / RECALL MADNESS / 8/22

Panel 5: LATINOS FINALLY HAVE A CANDIDATE WE CAN RALLY AROUND AND SUPPORT!! / RECALL MADNESS ©2003 LALO ALCARAZ

Panel 6: WOOHOO! GO **TERMINATOR**! **AHNOLD** FOR GUVERNATOR!! / HASTA LA VISTA BABY

©2003 LALO ALCARAZ /Dist. by Universal Press Syndicate

CANDIDACY FOR CALIFORNIA GOVERNOR DIDN'T WORK OUT / $ / 8/23

©2003 LALO ALCARAZ /Dist. by Universal Press Syndicate

122

HISPANIC HERITAGE MONTH IS COMING UP, HOMIE!

MUST YOU USE THE "H" WORD?

"HOMIE"?

NO, HISPANIC.

WHAT'S WRONG WITH "HISPANIC"?

WAY TOO EURO-CENTRIC. AND IT HAS THE WORD "PANIC" IN IT.

IT'S A TERM THE NIXON ADMINISTRATION CAME UP WITH TO LUMP ALL LATINOS TOGETHER.

OKAY, THEN HOW ABOUT "LATINO"?

THAT'S COOL, IF YOU'RE STILL SPEAKING LATIN...

©2003 LALO ALCARAZ /Dist. by Universal Press Syndicate

LALO ALCARAZ 8/24

I DON'T GET IT. WHY DO WE NEED SO MANY LABELS?

TO AVOID CONFUSION.

123

©2003 LALO ALCARAZ/Dist. by Universal Press Syndicate LALO ALCARAZ 8/25

GARY COLEMAN, SCHWARZENEGGER, ANGELYNE, LARRY FLYNT...

WHO ISN'T RUNNING FOR GOVERNOR OF CALIFORNIA?

CHEPE FOR GOVERNOR

PEPE FOR GOVERNOR "I'M THE MAN WHO CAN BEAT CHEPE"

LALO ALCARAZ 8/26 ©2003 LALO ALCARAZ/Dist. by Universal Press Syndicate

WHY ARE YOU GUYS EVEN RUNNING FOR OFFICE?

TO RESTORE DIGNITY TO POLITICS!

YOU MEAN CIVILITY!

DIGNITY!

CIVILITY!

CHEPE (D) FOR GOVERNOR

©2003 LALO ALCARAZ/Dist. by Universal Press Syndicate LALO ALCARAZ 8/27

CHEPE FOR GOVERNOR? WHAT'S THE "D" FOR?

THAT'S MY PARTY AFFILIATION.

"D" FOR DISORIENTED!

WHAT'S YOUR AFFILIATION, PEPE?

"I" FOR INDEPENDENT!

INCONTINENT?

I KNOW I AM, WHAT ARE YOU?!

CHEPE (D) FOR GOVERNOR

124

8/28

CUCO, WHO DO YOU THINK IS THE BEST CANDIDATE FOR GOVERNOR?

THAT'S TOUGH. WITH OVER 130 PEOPLE RUNNING...

I'D HAVE TO SAY... GARY COLEMAN!

HE'S GOT WHAT IT TAKES TO LEAD THE STATE OF CALIFORNIA IN A DIGNIFIED MANNER.

YOU'RE RIGHT! I'M VOTING FOR GARY COLEMAN!

THIS COMIC STRIP PAID FOR BY "FRIENDS OF GARY COLEMAN FOR GOVERNOR."

©2003 LALO ALCARAZ /Dist. by Universal Press Syndicate

8/29

I HATE SCHOOL UNIFORMS.

SO I AM EXPRESSING MY REBELLIOUS INDIVIDUALITY BY WEARING MY SPONGE-BOB T-SHIRT UNDERNEATH!

ME TOO!

©2003 LALO ALCARAZ /Dist. by Universal Press Syndicate

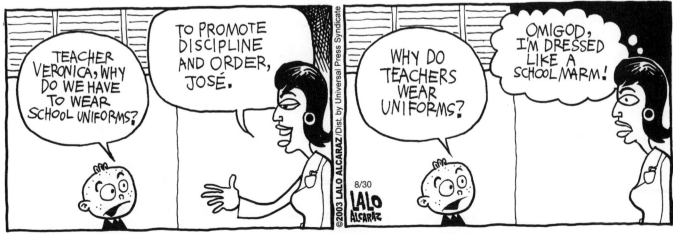

8/30

TEACHER VERONICA, WHY DO WE HAVE TO WEAR SCHOOL UNIFORMS?

TO PROMOTE DISCIPLINE AND ORDER, JOSÉ.

WHY DO TEACHERS WEAR UNIFORMS?

OMIGOD, I'M DRESSED LIKE A SCHOOLMARM!

©2003 LALO ALCARAZ /Dist. by Universal Press Syndicate

125

CUCO... IT'S ONE THING TO BUILD A SAND CASTLE...

AND IT'S OKAY TO MAKE IT A LARGE-SCALE REPLICA OF AN AZTEC PYRAMID...

BUT DO YOU REALLY HAVE TO LAUNCH MILITARY INVASIONS AGAINST THE OTHER SAND CASTLES?

SUBMIT, EVILDOER!

8/31

LALO ALCARAZ

©2003 LALO ALCARAZ /Dist. by Universal Press Syndicate

ARNOLD FOR GUVERNATOR

TIENDITA

I CAN'T BELIEVE THAT THE REPUBLICAN PARTY IS FINALLY EMBRACING IMMIGRANTS.

THEY SURE DO SEEM TO LOVE SCHWARZENEGGER.

OF COURSE IT DOESN'T HURT THAT HIS DADDY WAS A NAZI.

9/1 LALO ALCARAZ ©2003 LALO ALCARAZ /Dist. by Universal Press Syndicate

CHIEF OF HOMELAND SECURITY

OKAY, I CAN GET BEHIND THAT ONE.

JUMBO

9/2 LALO ALCARAZ ©2003 LALO ALCARAZ /Dist. by Universal Press Syndicate

WHY AREN'T YOU PEOPLE UP IN ARMS ABOUT THE LOSS OF CIVIL LIBERTIES?!

WE'RE UNDER SURVEILLANCE ALL THE TIME!

I SEE THE SIGNS EVERYWHERE!

FAUX NEWS

CUCO, YOU'RE JUST PARANOID.

I AM NOT.

THAT'S RIGHT. HE'S NOT.

FAIRLY IM-BALANCED

U.S. MAIL

9/3 LALO ALCARAZ ©2003 LALO ALCARAZ /Dist. by Universal Press Syndicate

127

©2003 LALO ALCARAZ /Dist by Universal Press Syndicate 9/4

PATRIOT ACT

I'M TELLIN' YA, THE SIGNS OF OPPRESSION ARE EVERYWHERE!

SHHHHH! I CAN'T HEAR THE COMIC!

I JUST ROLLED BACK CIVIL RIGHTS 50 YEARS... BOY ARE MY ARMS TIRED.

BUT SERIOUSLY, RAISE YOUR HANDS IF YOU DISAGREE WITH THE GOVERNMENT...

YOU'RE UNDER ARREST! DON'T YOU HATE WHEN THAT HAPPENS?

TOTAL INFORMATION AWARENESS*

AREN'T YOU THE LEAST BIT WORRIED ABOUT TOTAL INFORMATION AWARENESS?

NOT REALLY. WHAT IS IT?

*HAS BEEN CHANGED TO "TERRORIST INFORMATION AWARENESS."

IT'S A GOVERNMENT SPYING PROGRAM THAT COLLECTS INFORMATION ON EVERYONE, ALL THE TIME! T.I.A. IS A MENACE!

©2003 LALO ALCARAZ /Dist. by Universal Press Syndicate

T.I.A.? ARE YOU SURE YOU'RE NOT JUST TALKING ABOUT MY TIA "ROSIE LA NOSY"?

9/5

CITING THE DEFIANT INSTALLATION OF THE TEN COMMANDMENTS MONUMENT...

©2003 LALO ALCARAZ /Dist. by Universal Press Syndicate

ALABAMA STATE COURTHOUSE JANITOR HASSAM ALI JONES ERECTED A MONUMENT TO THE KORAN IN THE COURTHOUSE ROTUNDA.

9/6

IT WAS REMOVED FASTER THAN A PAIR OF LADIES' UNDERPANTS AT AN ENRIQUE IGLESIAS CONCERT.

128